PEMBROKE COLLEGE
CAMBRIDGE

PEMBROKE COLLEGE CAMBRIDGE

A CELEBRATION

Edited by A. V. Grimstone

Pembroke College, Cambridge

First published by Pembroke College,
Cambridge 1997
Copyright © The Master & Fellows of
Pembroke College, Cambridge

Designed and composed by Jeffery Design
Printed in England by BAS Printers, Over Wallop

Frontispiece The Foundress, Marie de St Pol,
Countess of Pembroke, kneeling. From a volume
containing Statutes of the University and of
Pembroke College, written *c.* 1629, purchased
by the Bibliothèque Royale, Paris in 1685.
(Paris, Bibliothèque National de France,
MS latin 4223B. Reproduced by permission.)

CONTENTS

PREFACE

This book has been produced on the occasion of the 650th anniversary of the College's foundation. As the sub-title implies, the intention has not been to produce a systematic history, which already exists, in preliminary form at least, in Attwater's *Pembroke College, Cambridge*, but rather to bring together essays, notes and illustrations that will combine to convey something of the life of a remarkable institution over six and a half centuries: people (famous and otherwise), buildings and the treasures that the College has accumulated over the years. The book has a chronological framework, each chapter covering roughly a century, but it will no doubt be dipped into rather than read as a continuous narrative. My hope is that it will be of interest both to old members of the College and to those newly entering Pembroke.

The book owes almost everything to friends and colleagues who have allowed themselves to be persuaded to write about their special fields of interest. With one exception, all are members of the College. Special thanks are due to Jayne Ringrose, College Archivist, who has written about the Foundress and the medieval College, and Peter Meadows, Architectural Archivist, who has provided much of the history of College buildings. Brian Watchorn has written an absorbing essay on perhaps the most important single group of Pembroke men, its early bishops; and Robert Douglas-Fairhurst, Richard McCabe and Colin Wilcockson have between them covered the major figures in the scarcely less notable company of Pembroke poets. Other contributions have come from Trevor Allan, Sidney Kenderdine, Michael Kuczynski, Charles Melville, Jonathan Parry and Jay Winter. The 650th anniversary coincides with the completion of the College's largest single building, and it is a particular pleasure to have an account of its planning and design from the architect, Eric Parry. To all of these I am deeply grateful. In a number of places it has proved possible to include material that has appeared previously in the *Pembroke College Cambridge Society Annual Gazette*, the 70 numbers of which are a mine of information about Pembroke. The illustrations constitute the most comprehensive collection of images of Pembroke and its possessions ever assembled. The majority of the photographs have been taken specially for the book by James Austin and readers will, I am sure, share my admiration of his skill.

A. V. G.

Acknowledgements

All but five of the illustrations depict the College and its possessions. The exceptions are the frontispiece, taken from a manuscript in the Bibliothèque National de France, figure 1, from the Foundress's breviary in Cambridge University Library, figure 47, from Serlio's *Architettura* in the Library of the Department of Architecture and History of Art, University of Cambridge, wgure 84, the portrait of Alfred Waterhouse in the National Portrait Gallery, and figure 95, which is a NASA photograph of Neptune. Thanks are due to all these institutions.

Figures 3 and 9 were drawn by John Rodford; figure 104 is adapted from drawings prepared by Eric Parry.

Most of the photography for this book was undertaken by James Austin. He was responsible for figures 1, 4–8, 12, 15–20, 25, 27, 29–31, 33, 35–40, 42–45, 49, 53–55, 57, 58, 60, 61, 65, 67, 69–76, 78, 80, 81, 83, 85–88, 90, 91, 93, 94, 99–101, 105–107, 109–112 and 116. Other photographs were provided by Ian Fleming (figures 114, 115 and 118), Robert Williams (figures 14 and 56) and *Country Life* Picture Library (figures 13, 46, 48 and 89). Photography of figures 1 and 21–23 was carried out by Cambridge University Library. Other illustrations come from the College's collections.

1 THE FOUNDRESS AND HER COLLEGE

Marie de St Pol

Benedicta igitur sit aula illa nobilis qua alumnus educatus sum et eius fundatrix devotissima domina Maria de sancto Paulo que cum Christo vivat in eternum deo gracias. 'Blessed therefore be that noble Hall, in which I was educated as a pupil, and its most devout Foundress, the Lady Mary of St. Pol; may she live with Christ in eternity; thanks be to God', wrote John Somerset (Pembroke, 1416), afterwards Chancellor of the Exchequer and physician to King Henry VI, in the copy of the *Canon* of Avicenna that he presented in 1448 to the College Library, to be chained in perpetuity. Matthew Wren was to record the gift, copying the inscription approvingly into his 1617 Library Benefactors Book (see p. 58), adding that it was well done and said (*'Bonum factum, dictumque'*). Manuscript 137 in the College collection has long parted with its chain but survives to bear witness to the extraordinary piety with which succeeding generations have regarded the woman who, in her forties, with much deliberation and the advice of a close-knit and trusted circle of advisers of her own choosing, founded a college of scholars in the University of Cambridge, to bear her name and her husband's.

She is at first sight an unlikely person to have begun such a project. She was born a French noblewoman, the fourth daughter of Guy of Châtillon, Count of St Pol, and his wife Mary, daughter of John, Earl of Richmond and Duke of Britanny, and was hence descended from a multiplicity of royal and noble families extending from England to Antioch. She was a great-niece of Edward I of England and a great-granddaughter of Henry III through her mother; both her maternal grandparents were descended from Henry II by different lines. In 1321 while still very young she had come to England as the second wife of Aymer de Valence, Earl of Pembroke, her third cousin, one of the then ten great earls in England and Wales, a powerful lord in the Welsh Marches and one of King Edward II's most trusted advisers. So great was the king's confidence in him that when Aymer briefly defected to the side of the king's

Breviary of the Foundress Marie de St Pol, Countess of Pembroke
(opposite)

Figure 1 From a breviary associated with the Foundress, perhaps to be identified with the volume left by her to her confessor and described in her will as 'my little breviary which the Queen [presumably the Queen of France] gave me'. The book was in Cambridge University Library by the mid-eighteenth century.

A breviary is an abbreviated form of the various volumes that, by the thirteenth century, were necessary for the recitation of divine service. It might be used in church or as a conveniently small volume for carrying on journeys. The Foundress's breviary is an outstanding example of fourteenth-century manuscript production, executed in the atelier of Jean Pucelle, the most renowned miniaturist in Paris. The numerous and vigorous marginal illustrations are characteristic of this atelier. Many pages bear the heraldic arms of Marie after her marriage to Aymer de Valence. The page illustrated shows the Foundress kneeling before St. Cecilia. (Cambridge University Library MS. Dd. 5. 5, f.388r. Reproduced by permission of the Syndics of Cambridge University Library.)

opponents and acted as custodian of the ill-starred royal favourite Piers Gaveston, Edward forgave him his part in the affair and presented him with Gaveston's hawks. It was Aymer who was with the king at the defeat of Bannockburn and who constantly travelled to France on royal diplomatic business. It was while he was in France on such a mission that, on 23 June 1324, he collapsed in the doorway upon rising from dinner and died, unconfessed, of apoplexy, in the arms of his servants. Such is the truth behind the romantic legend that he was killed at a tournament in celebration of his wedding, leaving Marie de St Pol maid, wife and widow in a day. The king sent his confessor Robert de Duffeld to the Countess at Hertford, probably to break the news. Her first concern was to secure a worthy funeral for her husband in Westminster Abbey, where his monument is still to be seen. She ordered black furs to wear in mourning to mark the end of a short married life of just under three years.

She was one of those proving Aymer's will in October. He had left debts, as a result of being held hostage in France in 1317; she had her widow's portion, but the earldom itself must be granted out afresh; her husband had political enemies among the nobility who could in turn make things difficult for her. From now on she must work to conserve her resources, and retrieve as much as she could of her dowry. Concerned to live well and safely, this for her seems to have meant in the long run the avoidance of both court life and re-marriage.

As a comparatively wealthy widow, she could live an independent life, retaining more control over her resources than a woman in any other state. Where Marie de St Pol differed from most was in her willingness to live chiefly surrounded by trusted members of her household. Significantly, one friend she did have of her own social status and whom she occasionally visited was her older contemporary Elizabeth de Burgh, Lady Clare, who took over and refounded University Hall as Clare College. There are several themes now in her life: an interest in the Franciscan order, the piety that focused on the proper commemoration of the departed, and an interest in the business side of what became her foundations. She must have picked up from her clerks, and by necessity in attempting to secure her widow's portion, a good working knowledge of how medieval business was done. She must have enjoyed securing benefices by papal provision to finance her clerks as they studied. Four entries in the earliest list of her College archives, drawn up in French during her lifetime, are annotated to imply that she retained documents in her custody for a while before handing them back to the new Master, Thomas Bingham, in 1365. One, a papal bull (figure 2), is clearly stated to be 'en la garde madame' when the list was first drawn up.

We should not think of her as a recluse. She travelled in France a good deal and was to direct that in admissions to her College

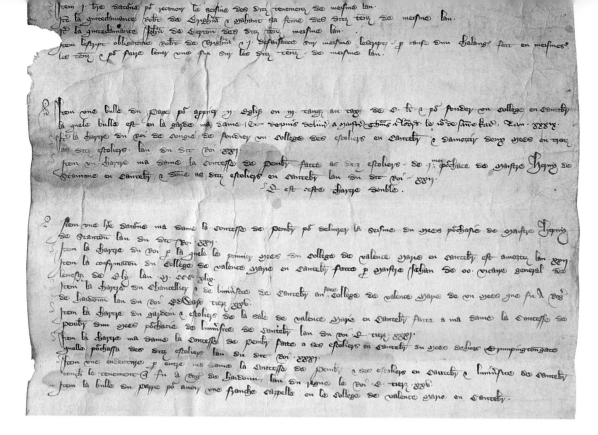

Figure 2 An early list of the College archives, in French, drawn up before 1365. The first line of the second paragraph refers to a papal bull, which is said to be in the keeping of the Foundress ('en la garde madame'), for appropriating the revenues of churches to the College. (This particular bull survives only as copied into the great register.) An added note states that it was given to 'maistre Thomas a Londres le jour de sainte Kat[herine] Lan xxxix'. (Master Thomas is probably Thomas de Bingham, Master from 1364; the date is 25 November in the 39th year of Edward III, i.e. 1365.) Below this is an entry for the College's Foundation Charter. (College Archives, College Box A6.)

preference was to be given to Frenchmen. She was not excused from sending troops for the siege of Calais in 1347 and, as a friend of the old Queen Isabel, she was apparently working for good relations between England and France in the 1350s. In 1361 she was among those of the nobility, including many ladies, summoned by the king to attend a Council to provide for the better defence of Ireland. She moved her household frequently between her various residences, her particular favourites being Anstey Castle and the manor of La Mote at Cheshunt, both in Hertfordshire, and Great Braxted in Essex, where her will is dated.

Throughout her life, Marie showed a constant interest in the Franciscan order, as her College statutes and her will, for example, show. Her household had its own confessor, John de Peverel, a Franciscan friar, and on her return from France in the 1330s she turned her attention to the community of Franciscan nuns at Waterbeach, near Cambridge, which had been founded in 1293 by Denise de Munchensi, a relation of her husband. In 1327 Marie had acquired the manor of Denny (between Cambridge and Ely) and intended to confer it upon the nuns, but by 1339 she had gone further and decided to transfer the whole community to the new site, where there was already a religious house, originally a cell of Ely Priory: it was a drier site than Waterbeach. She accordingly obtained the licence to transfer the nuns to Denny, and apparently wished to place Franciscan friars on the old site. Nothing came of the latter intention but the transfer of the nuns did take place. This seems not to have been entirely popular with them: some apparently had to be removed from Waterbeach by force. They were finally established in 1351 at what was to become Denny Abbey, literally as the College or Hall of Valence Marie (i.e. Pembroke) was being founded. These Minoresses or Poor Clares of Denny were one of only three communities of the mitigated Franciscan rule in England. Their rule, less austere than the original one, allowed each nun to have a servant. The other two houses were in London (in what was afterwards called the Minories) and in Bruisyard in Suffolk, which was originally established with nuns from Denny in 1364. All three houses appear in the Foundress's will, and she was a frequent visitor to Denny, where she would have travelled with her servants, including her servant-companion for over fifty years, Mabel du Bois. Her scholars at her new college were directed to be good to Franciscans, who were well established in the University and whose privileges and exemptions often gave rise to ill-feeling among secular clerks. It was at Denny that, in 1377, the Foundress was buried, in the Franciscan habit, in the tomb that had been made for her.

The idea of founding a college in Cambridge may have come to her quite late, since she seems to have been undecided throughout the early 1340s, and even to have toyed with the idea of a monastic foundation. It may be that, after her difficulties with the nuns at Denny, she wanted something that she could control, experiment with and change – as her two codes of College statutes suggest – and that would also interact directly with her household of clerks. It should come as no surprise to us to learn that of the two proctors sent by her College to the papal court at Avignon to negotiate on the College's behalf in respect of its livings and advowsons, one, Rayner d'Ambonnay (two of whose letters of commission, dated 1359, survive) was rector of the Church of St Florence in Pembrokeshire, doubtless on her own appointment, and the other, Robert de Stanton, was a Franciscan friar. Other reasons for her turning to the idea of founding a college can only be guessed at. Her friendship with Lady Clare and perhaps with Edmund Gonville, who assisted her with the acquisition of land for the College site and makes brief appearances in the early deeds of the College, may have been influential. There is no evidence in the Foundress's life of an inspirational figure comparable to John Fisher (who inspired Lady Margaret Beaufort to found Christ's College and, as one of her executors, was instrumental in founding her second college of St John's), no-one to seek her patronage as Andrew Docket had sought that of two Queens for his foundation of Queens' College and no existing College that we know of in need of help. But she knew two of the founders of the early colleges and she was a dear cousin of

The Arms of Pembroke College

Figure 3 The College's coat of arms is formed by halving the coats of arms of the Foundress and her husband, Aymer de Valence and putting the two halves together. (They are said to be *dimidiated* and *conjoined*.) The arms of the Foundress are on the right, those of Valence on the left.

VALENCE. Hugh de Lusignan, who married our King John's widow, bore simply 'burely silver and azure' (A). *Burely* means striped horizontally, the number of stripes being indefinite, varying with the scale and technique used. William, his second son, took the name of Valence from a place in Poitou, and differenced his arms by putting over the stripes a red orle. An *orle* is a kind of border following the outline of the shield, a little way in from the edge. Afterwards, when he married an heiress of the Earls of Pembroke, he made this into a red orle of martlets, a *martlet* being a kind of swallow supposed never to alight and there-fore drawn without feet. They are not set on or between the stripes but at regular intervals to make the half orle. The same coat was borne by his son Aylmer de Valence, husband of the Foundress (B).

CHÂTILLON. The main branch of the Châtil-lons bore their coat as seen in C, taken from the seal of John, Count of Blois, elder brother of Guy, the Foundress's father: 'red, three pales vair, a chief gold'. A *pale* is a vertical strip; *vair* is the fur of a grey squirrel conventionally represented by a chequer of shield-shaped patches alternately blue and white to give the effect of its dark back and light belly. On a pale there is room for one vertical row of such 'shields'. A *chief* is the upper third of a shield. Guy as Count of St Pol in Picardy put an azure label across the gold chief (D, from the Foundress's seal), a *label* being a narrow horizontal strip from which hang tabs or 'points', which can be rectangular or like dovetails.

The formal description of the whole coat of arms is therefore:

Burely silver and azure, an orle of martlets red, for VALENCE:
Red, three pales vair, on a chief gold a label of five points azure, for
ST POL DE CHATILLON:
The whole dimidiated and conjoined.

The College bears its arms by prescription, not by grant: they appear upon its original seal. It does not bear any crest: ladies do not bear crests, so the Foundress could not have transmitted one. Further, corporate bodies did not begin to bear them for more than a century after her time, and the College has never adopted the doubtful practice, so a martlet should not be put above the College arms.

(Adapted from an article by Sir Ellis Minns, *PCCS Annual Gazette*, **14** (1940).)

Figure 4 The Foundation Charter of the College. Letters patent dated 24 December 1347 at Guildford, and bearing the Privy Seal of Edward III. The king has granted to his dear cousin, Mary of St Pol, Countess of Pembroke that she may found a house of scholars in the town of Cambridge. (College Archives, College Box A1.)

Edward III, who had already established the King's Hall in Cambridge for his own clerks in 1337. Founding a college would provide a fitting memorial and means of commemoration for herself and her husband, as the name she first gave it, the Hall of Valence Marie, shows. At the same time it would offer a constant source of personal interest: an extension of her own household and a means of charity, of providing for the welfare of just the sort of people with whom she liked to surround herself. When she made her will shortly before her death the clerks she named as her executors included John de Tynmouth, Fellow and afterwards Master of the College.

The early foundation and statutes

The letters patent of Christmas Eve 1347 (figure 4) provided for Marie de St Pol to found a house of thirty scholars in the town of Cambridge. The same document empowered her to confer on them up to three messuages of land (i.e. building plots) in the town, and advowsons to the value of one hundred pounds, notwithstanding

Figure 5 The Statutes of the College in book form, written out after the Foundress's death (i.e. after 1377). The book originally bore two seals on silk strings, one (now lost) of the University and one of the College. There is a second, plainer copy of these statutes in the University Archives. (College Archives, College Box A12.)

mortmain. There probably never were as many as thirty scholars together at any point in her lifetime, or long afterwards: Wren recorded nine ('and one boy') in 1412 and ten in 1469, but the three messuages of land (two for the first court and one for the garden) were gradually accumulated (see p. 13) and the three advowsons of Tilney and Saxthorpe in Norfolk, and Waresley in Huntingdonshire were conferred and established as College livings, their tithes being appropriated to the College, who paid and appointed a vicar, almost always chosen from the Fellowship.

A picture of early College life can be gained from the two texts of College statutes that survive, both claiming to have been drawn up by the Foundress in 1347 but both plainly written out after her death in 1377, since they refer to her as being of illustrious memory. The earlier one described a college on what is usually termed the Parisian model, with two external rectors, one to be a Franciscan, both elected by the Fellows, to act as a last resort in the settling of disputes at the request of the Master and Fellows, to confirm the election of the Fellows and in certain circumstances to expel them. This may have made the College too self-governing for the Foundress's liking; in both versions, she reserved to herself the power to interpret or change the statutes according to her own judgement, and in the later document, which makes no mention of rectors, she reserved to herself the right to admit and expel Fellows. Behaviour likely to prove unacceptable included drunkenness, the frequenting of taverns and 'dishonest spectacles', contentiousness, lechery and notable viciousness (undefined); also the revealing of secrets of the house or anything that, if known, might cause scandal.

Both codes must have been drawn up in consultation with an expert in University procedure and business. The College was founded, according to the preamble, for the honour of our Lord Jesus Christ, the advancement of Holy Mother Church, and the augmentation of the clergy and of study. Of the thirty planned Fellows, twenty-four were to be major scholars, or fellows, studying arts and theology, while six were to be minor scholars, *grammatici* (first- and second-year undergraduates whose course was dominated by grammar and logic) or *sophiste* (third and fourth years, concentrating on natural philosophy and beginning to take part in disputations). This reflects the medieval Cambridge curriculum. With the exception of the privileged religious orders, who were excused it, those wishing to study theology had first to take the full arts course, which involved four years for the BA and a further three years mainly of philosophy with some mathematics for the MA. Of the major scholars, a fixed proportion were to be in priest's orders. Upon graduating in arts, Fellows were expected to move on to theology (although some canon law could be studied ancillary to this). It is plain that the Foundress did not want her clerks given over to the study of canon law, which was to attract so many with the hope of worldly advantage in the Church.

All were to present to the College a surplice, mazer (drinking bowl), spoon, napkin (*mappa*) and handtowel approved by the treasurers; clothing of a uniform design was provided by the house. They were to share two to a room (except for the Master), eat together and speak Latin, or at any rate French if possible, and refrain from murmuring. The earlier code is fierce about parties; these were evidently popular on saints' days, such as St William of York, or St Hugh of Lincoln, or on going up or coming down. The Williams and Hughs who wished to give parties had to give them to their table fellows only; guests from outside College were not encouraged. There was careful regulation of the giving of presents of robes, tabards or gloves to University dignitaries at graduations. Limits were set to graduation parties and all debts had to be settled within a fortnight of going down.

Teaching in medieval Cambridge was by lecture and by hearing or joining in disputations; wits were sharpened by practice in debating all sides of a question. In the statutes, elaborate arrangements were laid down to ensure that every bachelor and sophist had a turn in disputations held in the College hall, where all, seniors and juniors, were to be present. At the regular disputations for the artists, for example, two questions a fortnight were disputed, one a sophism or logical question and one a question in natural philosophy. Examination was also largely by disputation: there were what we should call mock examinations and extra practice in disputing for those due to respond in the Schools on Ash Wednesday, when the series of formal university acts leading ultimately to the BA began.

The Foundress's keen interest in administration appears in the regulations for the chest for money, the muniments and other treasures of the house and the common seal. The great seal (figure 6), which she gave to the College and which is appended to the later code of the statutes, shows a figure with a cross in the nimbus,

Figure 6 In the process of acquiring the second plot of land for the College site, the College grants it temporarily back to the Foundress, 20 August 1357. The original College seal, granted by the Foundress, shows her with Aymer de Valence supporting the original building (perhaps the Chapel) with Christ enthroned upon the roof. Beside it is the original matrix of this seal. (College Archives, College Box c6.)

Figure 7 The College's secret seal, '*sigillum nostrum securum*', depicting the Holy Trinity; the seated figure of God the Father supports the Crucifix. (The Dove, representing the Holy Spirit, which might be expected, is frequently omitted in such depictions, in this case probably for reasons of space.) Attached to an acquittance to Sir Lawrence Barkley for 20s. in part payment for the rent of half a manor of Morchall at Whissendine in Rutland, 1 May 1437. (College Archives, Wissenden c6.)

Figure 8 The personal large seal of the Foundress, showing her standing above a peacock; from the document granting the first plot of the site (see. p 13) to the College, 9 June 1348. Beside it is the Foundress's secret seal, with her own arms surrounded by those of England, France and Dreux (her grandfather John of Dreux was Duke of Brittany); from her letter of attorney to her chaplain Richard Pickering to deliver seisin to the College (i.e. formally handing over possession) of the first plot, 10 June 1348. (College Archives, College Box B7.)

probably intended to represent Christ, seated above a building with a bell-turret, conventionally representing the new chapel, which is in turn supported by the outstretched hands of Aymer de Valence and Marie, and beside them their coats of arms. On the back of this example is an impression of the College's small round secret seal, which bears an image of the Holy Trinity. That this was the dedication of the College is corroborated by documentary evidence in the archives, and by the papal indulgence secured by the Foundress in 1374 for all those attending and contributing to the chapel, which she founded in the name and honour of the Holy Trinity, on certain feasts. All sealed documents were to be entered into a register. Flexibility was shown in the provisions concerning money. There was an awareness of rising prices and the Fellows' allowances varied with the market price of corn.

The great days for auditing and election or re-election to office in the earlier statutes were St Denys' day (9 October), because it was the day before the University year began, and the feast of St Thomas Becket (7 July), because it was the day after the University year ended; or the following week. The book audit was carried out on the latter day, and the early statutes provide a remarkable account of a borrowing register, consisting of a set of boards with the titles of the books written on a narrow strip of parchment pasted down one side; these boards were divided vertically, so that flanking the parchment was a column of wax, on which to write the borrower's name temporarily against the relevant title. The elaborate book audit, and other elections of 7 July disappear in the later code, which seems more aware of the need for change in response to circumstances.

What does not change between the codes, of course, is the requirement to commemorate the Foundress, whether alive or dead, Aymer de Valence, and the parents of both of them; for it is the duty of those who benefit to return favour to their benefactors. Their names were to be inserted into every mass, and there were individual masses on their anniversaries as well as the recitation of the office for the dead on Fridays and a regular requiem on Saturdays. A special mass was held on the 3rd or 4th of July for the souls of Mabel du Bois, the Foundress's companion and servant, also of Rayner d'Ambonnay and Robert de Stanton, the College's two emissaries to the papal court at Avignon. The commemoration programme was not as onerous as that of some other colleges, but as time went on further provision was made for the commemoration of deceased Fellows and benefactors, including benefactors to come. Finally, the Fellows were to give aid and counsel to the sisters at Denny, especially in business matters. There is some evidence that this was more than a formality.

Jayne Ringrose

2 THE MEDIEVAL COLLEGE

Pembroke is the earliest Cambridge college to survive today on its original site with an unbroken constitution from its first foundation. It prospered from the outset, rapidly acquiring land and putting in place what are still the essential elements of a college: chapel, library, hall and accommodation for Master, Fellows and students. It early acquired a reputation in theology, which would in time lead to the College's long line of bishops (see Chapter 3). Pembroke men also came to play important roles in affairs of state and were able to secure for the College the patronage of Henry VI. Within the context of the medieval University as a whole, Pembroke appears as a college well constituted and equipped for development and survival.

The College site

The modern College site, approximately five acres in extent, was built up slowly in a series of purchases made over a period of about five hundred years (figure 9). It will be simplest to deal with the whole site in this chapter, even though many of the acquisitions lay far in the future.

The first three plots were acquired by the Foundress herself between 1346 and 1363. The first was a strip of land extending from Trumpington Street along the King's Ditch (now the line of Pembroke Street) to the east end of what is now Ivy Court (1). As was usual with town building plots at the time, it was long and narrow. This was bought from Hervey de Stanton, Rector of Elm, near Wisbech. Five years later a second plot (2), adjacent to the first and called University Hostel was bought from the Chancellor, Regents and non-Regents of the University (figure 6). These two purchases gave the land needed for the first small court of which the College originally consisted (see p. 17), as well as the north side of Ivy Court.

To the south and east of the early College there was an extensive open pasture called Swynecroft or St Thomas' Leys, which stretched from Trumpington Street to the modern Regent Street. As her third and final purchase, the Foundress bought an acre of Swynecroft (3) and made it into an orchard, thereby extending the College site up to what later became Tennis Court Road. In 1401 this extension was added to by purchase of a further large piece of ground (5), to the south of the orchard, the two together becoming the Fellows' Garden. However, these new acquisitions were separated from the rest of the site by a lane, often termed the *venella* in latin documents, which gave public access to Swynecroft from the north. (The path that today crosses the east end of Ivy Court and continues towards the library is a fragment of this lane.) It would take over 200 years to eliminate this division of the site.

Enlargement of the site along Trumpington Street continued after the Foundress's death with the purchase of two more narrow plots, parallel to the first two: Cosyn's Place in 1389 (4) and Bolton's or Knapton's Place in 1430 (6). These were not contiguous and the ground between them (8), belonging to a chantry in Little St Mary's church, was not acquired until 1549. Further extension southward along Trumpington Street came about in 1451 by the leasing in perpetuity from the Hospital of St John the Evangelist of a tenement called St Thomas' Hostel (7). Used initially for the housing of students, this was demolished in 1662 to make way for the building of the new chapel. The site now consisted of a roughly rectangular block of land between Trumpington Street and Pembroke Street,

Figure 9 Plan showing the development of the College site, based on the one in Willis & Clark, *Architectural history of the University of Cambridge*. The outlines of modern buildings are superimposed.

1 Messuage (i.e. building plot) of Hervey de Stanton, 1346.
2 University Hostel, 1351.
3 An acre of Swynecroft, 1363.
4 Cosyn's Place, 1389.
5 Three roods in Swynecroft, 1401.
6 Bolton's or Knapton's Place, 1430.
7 St Thomas' Hostel, 1451.
8 Chantry belonging to Little St Mary's church, 1549.
9 Paschal Yard, leased 1609, purchased 1833.
10 The *venella*, closed 1659, leased 1668.
11 Crossinge Place, 1737.
12 Waste ground, bought from town, 1832.
13 Exchange with Peterhouse, 1854.
14 St Peter's Close, bought from Peterhouse, 1861.

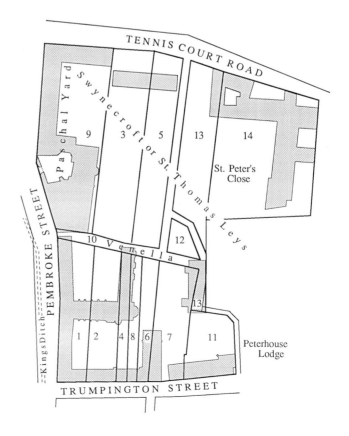

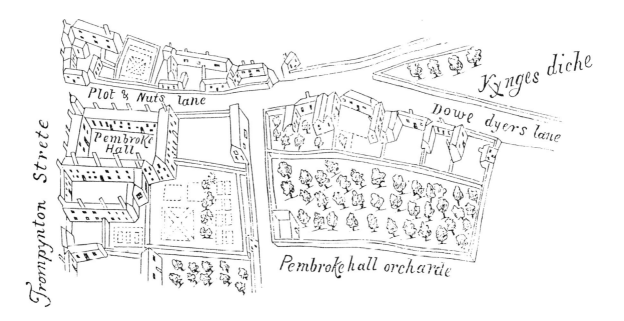

Figure 10 Detail from Hammond's map of Cambridge (1592), redrawn by Willis & Clark, showing the land bought by the Foundress (3 in figure 9) to form an orchard. Old Court is shown, with the chapel's western turret.

large enough to accommodate the present First Court, Ivy Court and the present chapel, together with the orchard and adjacent land (the Fellows' Garden) to the east.

The next acquisition was a large plot (9) north of the Fellows' Garden which filled in the north-eastern corner of the site (between the present Pembroke Street and Tennis Court Road), where New Court, the old Master's Lodge and Pitt Building now stand. Known as Paschal Yard, this land had originally belonged to a chantry in Great St Mary's church, the name deriving from its leases being used in part to provide a Paschal candle in that church. It had subsequently passed to Corpus Christi College, from whom it was leased in 1609 and eventually purchased in 1833.

The site was still divided by the *venella* (10) running from Pembroke Street to the remainder of Swynecroft. This lane, six yards wide, was big enough to take a horse and cart. The inconvenience of this arrangement was addressed in 1618, when the College opened negotiations with the town for enclosure of the lane. A lease for 500 years was granted in 1620, which provided that a public footpath must be kept open in daytime and the College must make another lane giving access to Swynecroft 'out of the lane leading down from Emmanuel College' (i.e. what is now Pembroke Street) along the east edge of the Fellows' Garden. This lane eventually became Tennis Court Road. The College effectively closed off the *venella* when the south range of Ivy Court was built in 1659, a state of affairs regularised in a new lease granted in 1668.

Houses where Red Buildings now stands (11) were bought in 1737,

Figure 11 Photograph of about 1870, showing Old Court from the main gate. The north range (left) is much as it is today. The medieval Hall and the south range were demolished in the 1870s.

using part of the money bequeathed by Richard Crossinge, Fellow, thus completing the western part of the site along Trumpington Street. It remained to extend the site towards the south. The present avenue that runs from Tennis Court Road towards the chapel corresponds roughly in position to a lane that ran under the wall of the Fellows' Garden to meet the *venella*. A triangular patch of waste ground at its west end was leased from the town in 1804 and purchased in 1832 (12). Swynecroft having been enclosed in 1803 by Act of Parliament, all the various lanes were now closed to the public. The lane just mentioned was continued towards Peterhouse Master's Lodge stables, for the convenience of both colleges.

Two further transactions, both with Peterhouse, made under Gilbert Ainslie's energetic mastership, completed the College site. In 1854, as part of an exchange, Peterhouse ceded a piece of ground south of the Fellows' Garden, including the adjoining lane, and a small triangular plot on which the Library is now partly built (13). In 1861 Pembroke bought from Peterhouse the large plot, St Peter's Close (14), which until recently contained the 1933 Master's Lodge and the modern Fellows' Garden. It is on this land that the new building has just been erected.

A. V. Grimstone

The medieval buildings

OLD COURT

The original College consisted of a single court, long known as Old Court, occupying about half the space of the present First Court. It was substantially complete by 1389. Built on the first two pieces of land acquired by the Foundress, Old court was consequently small and narrow and remained so until its south range was demolished in 1874. Loggan's view of 1681 (figure 39, p. 54), the plan in figure 63 (p. 82) and the photograph dating from about 1870 (figure 11) between them give an impression of Old Court.

The College was entered, as now, from Trumpington Street, through an arched gateway with the arms of the Foundress and the Royal Arms above, flanked by two oriel windows (figure 12). This is probably an original arrangement, not found elsewhere in Cambridge colleges, but now somewhat masked behind eighteenth-century stone facing. The present Royal Arms, dating from the time of the facing, are those of George I.

In the east range, the Hall was separated from the kitchen by a screens passage, which led into a garden in what is now Ivy Court.

Figure 12 The main gateway from Trumpington Street. This retains its medieval form but was encased in ashlared stone in the eighteenth century.

At the south-east corner the Master had his chambers. Other rooms, for Fellows and students, filled the south, west and part of the north ranges. At the north-west corner of the court was the chapel, now the Old Library.

THE CHAPEL

Pembroke was the first Cambridge college to have its own chapel. The Foundress at first intended to use St Botolph's church, but she later obtained licences from Pope Innocent V (1355), Bishop Simon Langham of Ely (1365) and Pope Urban V (1366) to found a chapel, with turret and bells, and to have a chaplain. Masonry from this original chapel is probably incorporated in the walls of the present Old Library, though hidden beneath the stone facing. A fragment of the old chapel, a piscina, was found during building work in 1879 and installed in the sanctuary of the Wren chapel.

To the east of the chapel was the vestry, and in 1398 Bishop Fordham licensed the celebration of Mass there. The room above (now called the Christopher Smart Room (E5), though previously known as the President's Room) was probably the chaplain's chamber. In this there are the remains of a window, which once looked into the chapel, and part of a circular structure, which was either a staircase or possibly a bell-turret east of the chapel. Matthew Wren, who read College archives now lost, recorded that the bell turret was not built until 1436 but did not note its position. Hammond's map of Cambridge (1592; figure 10) shows a turret at the west end of the chapel, and Loggan's engraving (p. 54) shows a western belfry. Loggan shows also the five-light west window provided by the Master, Robert Swinburne, in 1536. The side windows are not shown: they were given stained glass in 1463 by Laurence Booth, Master 1450–80. Richard Parker in his history of Cambridge (1623) records that they all contained Booth's coat of arms.

Booth also gave stalls, a rood-screen and loft, and figures of saints and doctors of the Church. This was probably in 1475, when Matthew Wren records that the choir of the chapel was completely re-done. The stalls and screen provided models for woodwork which Robert Shorton, a Pembroke graduate and first Master of St John's College, gave to his new chapel. The carpenter's contract specified stalls 'according to the seats within the Qwyer of Pembroke Hall . . . and a Rodeloft . . . according to the Roodelofte and Candell beame in the said Pembroke Hall . . . with imagery and howsing'. Shorton's stalls are still in St John's chapel and his screen is now in Whissendine church, Rutland.

The sixteenth-century Reformation brought the abolition of the Mass and with it the loss of chapel service-books and textiles.

Figure 13 Doorway of the Old Library (early seventeenth century).

Fifteenth-century inventories record the richness of the chapel's fittings. There was a high altar, two lower altars, an altar in the vestibule (which then extended back to Trumpington Street) and another in the vestry. There were at least twenty-two sets of vestments, some embroidered with the Foundress's arms or those of other donors; nine or more copes, many altar frontals, canopies and so forth. There were brass crosses, candelabra, thuribles and censers. Two chalices were kept in the vestry and were doubtless of silver. Amongst the books were nine missals, thirteen antiphoners and nine grails. None of these chapel furnishings and textiles has survived. Many of them are listed in an inventory drawn up for Cardinal Pole's commissioners in 1556, during the restoration of Roman Catholicism in Queen Mary's reign. They must have been discarded in the reign of her successor Queen Elizabeth, when the silver chalices were replaced by two communion cups. The College archives contain lists of books, with annotations that they were sold and new service books in English bought to replace them.

The Chapel's decoration was largely intact until the 1640s. Extra seating was provided in 1619, near the altar, presumably in space left by the removal of the screen. About that time the chapel door in the court was renewed, in oak, with carvings of a pilaster and a cherub (now the door into the Old Library, figure 13). The iconoclast William Dowsing arrived in Cambridge in December 1643 to purge chapels of superstitious imagery. The Fellows made a spirited defence of the chapel but Dowsing, armed with a Parliamentary commission, overcame them and broke down ten cherubim and eighty 'superstitious pictures', possibly the stained glass windows.

No trace remains of a separate chapel built by John Langton about 1430. Matthew Wren (1622) noted 'that elegant little chapel for the Master, under which is a room . . . in which the poor scholars take their meals', and Richard Parker mentioned it in 1623, but neither writer said where it was. It was probably part of the Master's Lodge, not too far from the Hall and kitchen, if food was to be taken there. Perhaps it projected into Ivy Court, on the site of the present Hitcham building.

THE LIBRARY AND HALL

Figure 14 (opposite) Panelling from the old Hall, now above the fireplace at the high table end of the Hall.

The Foundress provided in early statutes for a librarian but the location of the original Library is uncertain. There is still today a large first-floor room at what would have been the south-west corner of the Old Court, double height, with a tall Gothic window looking on to Trumpington Street. Perhaps the College library was originally here. However, a fifteenth-century College document calls this room simply the 'great chamber'. In 1417 twenty-two chains were bought for books and in 1436 the glass of the library window was mended. By the early part of the fifteenth century the library, wherever it was, was becoming too small. Through the influence of John Langton, chaplain to Henry VI, a letter was sent to the King requesting him to grant timber for a new library, which was in due course built over the Hall.

The Hall was originally a single-storey building with a pitched roof. It was small, but adequate for a society that until the 1870s rarely numbered more than a dozen Fellows and forty students. In 1452 the roof was removed and a flat ceiling installed; above it Laurence Booth built a new library. In 1634 the Hall was renovated, with new panelling and carved screens, much of which is now at the high table end of the present Hall (figure 14). A classical doorcase was added at the screens entrance in Old Court (see Loggan, p. 54). This was moved in 1863 to the entrance to the garden from Ivy Court (figure 15). Loggan shows Gothic tracery in the Hall windows, but not accurately enough to date it precisely.

Gateway, Pembroke College   30/80   *Richard Sell 1964*

Figure 15 Doorcase from old Hall, now at
the entrance to the garden from Ivy Court.
Lithograph by Richard Sell, 1964.

THE MASTER'S QUARTERS

Before the Reformation the Master was an unmarried priest and the Master's Lodge consisted of only a couple of rooms, to the south of the Hall. The ground-floor room was the Parlour or Fellows' Combination Room; above it was a room called the Audit Room, where College Meetings were held, and which the Master used as a dining room. The rooms were linked by a spiral staircase at the south-east corner of Old Court, which after 1452 gave access also to the Library. After 1549, when the purchase of Little St Mary's chantry land (8 in figure 9) allowed the site south of Old Court to be completed, the Master's quarters were extended south. The Master could now marry and might have children.

Peter Meadows

Good and worshipful clerks

During the fifteenth century Pembroke became extremely successful in producing the 'good and worshipful clerkis' to whom Queen Margaret of Anjou referred in her formal request to Henry VI to permit the foundation of Queens' College. Pembroke was founded at a time of rapid collegiate development. The small and varied hostels in which students had lodged hitherto would continue in existence until well into the sixteenth century, but Pembroke's acquisition in 1451 of St Thomas's Hostel, with a Pembroke Fellow acting as its Exterior Principal, was an example of a process whereby colleges often took over these institutions as subsidiaries and eventually replaced them.

Other developments which were also to become normative in the Cambridge that we know today can be traced in Pembroke at an early stage. The system whereby Fellows acted as tutors to individual pupils assigned to them, first found at the King's Hall, and which eventually grew into the tutorial system as we now have it, was operating in Pembroke certainly in the 1470s, when Fellows were obliged to pay the room rents of their pupils, the second earliest reference to such a practice in Cambridge. Cambridge colleges had already begun to act as lodgings for mature 'commoners': ex-fellows, clergy or graduates who resided, perhaps for a refresher course of study, to take an advanced degree, or for social reasons. Pembroke had its share of these, but it was in the forefront of new developments in taking undergraduate commoners (who would otherwise have lived in hostels) to reside in college under a paid tutor. Hitherto, only minor scholars on the foundation could be undergraduates in college. College lecturing also developed about this time: a theology lectureship was founded at Pembroke in 1507–8 by Sir John Hussey, Comptroller of the Royal Household.

Figure 16 Medieval bench from old Hall, still in use.

Meanwhile, Pembroke men were already enjoying Royal favour outside the College. John Langton, Fellow in 1412 and Master in 1428, was Chancellor of the University from 1436 and, together with John Somerset (at Pembroke from 1416, afterwards Chancellor of the Exchequer) and the canon lawyer William Lyndewode, was responsible for carrying out Henry VI's foundation of King's College. Langton was the donor of a number of books, and died as Bishop of St David's in 1447. Somerset migrated to Cambridge from Oxford and rose to favour as Henry VI's physician.

A notable strand in the College's early history was an ever-growing connection with the north of England. Laurence Booth (Master, 1450–80) was elected Archbishop of York in 1476. A great man in church and state (he was Chancellor of England from July 1473 until his dismissal in 1474), he took refuge from the political situation and resided in Pembroke during the 1460s, to the College's great advantage. Booth's benefactions to Pembroke are touched on below: he was also active in strengthening the establishment of the Fellows. On his death the College elected as Master his successor as Archbishop of York, Thomas Rotherham. Rotherham is famous as a benefactor of the University Library and for completing the University's Schools buildings, which Booth had begun. He gave Pembroke books that it still possesses, but he was to found his own institution, Jesus College Rotherham, and was not a major benefactor to Pembroke.

In the fourteenth century, Pembroke was one of the three leading colleges for theology, along with Michaelhouse (later a component, with the King's Hall and others, of Trinity College) and Gonville Hall. Other colleges would follow suit and Pembroke, in turn, would produce a modest number of canon and civil lawyers, but so great was Pembroke's reputation as a nursery of orthodox theologians that by the late fifteenth and early sixteenth century other colleges constantly drew upon its members. Edward Storey, Fellow by 1446, was Master of Michaelhouse in 1466, and Chancellor of the University in 1471, dying as Bishop of Chichester. Thomas Langton, Fellow of Pembroke from 1461, eventually became Provost of the Queen's College, Oxford. In 1501, by then Bishop of Winchester, he was elected Archbishop of Canterbury but died before he could be translated. He was the donor of the Anathema Cup (figure 17) and bequeathed vestments and money. Richard Stubbes, a member and possibly a Fellow of Pembroke, became Master of Clare College in 1487; William Chubbes, a Fellow from 1466, became the first Master of Jesus College in 1497, and Robert Shorton, Fellow of Jesus College in 1503 migrated to Pembroke as Fellow in 1505 and became the first Master of St John's, 1511, returning to Pembroke as Master in 1516. This home of good and worshipful clerks was to produce numerous Reformers during the early sixteenth century.

Meanwhile, Pembroke continued to be a favourite place in which to reside: such evidence as survives suggests a place of convivial friendship as well as good learning. Thomas Anlaby of North Ferriby in Yorkshire gave a number of books to Pembroke Hall where he 'sogernd and lernyd', perhaps in the late 1420s. A man of substance, he compiled a cartulary of his estates before 1450 (now Fitzwilliam Museum MS. 329), in which he records his gifts to the College, one of which (Aquinas) he says he handed over in 1458 to Mr Gerard Skipwith to be chained in the Library for the use of the Fellows there studying. This particular book does not survive, but Gerard Skipwith is well documented. He and his brother Nicholas were both admitted as Fellows around 1450. Gerard held the living of Eltisley in Huntingdonshire, in the gift of Denny Abbey from 1465, and also rented a field from the nuns. He gave the College lands and books: Pembroke MS. 255 is in his own taut clear hand.

Figure 17 The Anathema Cup. The cup bears a (Latin) inscription in black letter: '*T. Langton Bishop of Winchester formerly Fellow of Pembroke Hall gave this covered cup to the said Hall, 1497. Who shall alienate it let him be anathema lxvii oz.*'

The cup weighs 39 oz. so the lost cover (sent to King Charles) must have weighed 28 oz. It is described in a College inventory as having six pinnacles at the top. The curse no doubt saved the cup itself. It is one of the largest surviving examples of its kind and takes apart in the middle for packing. The nearest analogue is the gold and enamel cup of the Kings of France (now in the British Museum). The date mark, 1481/2, is the fourth earliest known. The maker's mark, described as a 'fetter lock', is unique and unidentified.

Given in 1497 by Thomas Langton, D.D., Fellow 1461, afterwards Provost of the Queen's College, Oxford, Bishop of Winchester and Archbishop designate of Canterbury (d. 1500).

If Gerard Skipwith was a good college man in touch with the nuns of Denny, so was Richard Sokborn, Fellow from 1470–79. Vicar of the College living of Soham from 1479, he gave the College handsome presents of silver, including probably the silver-gilt mazer that was afterwards known as the Foundress's Cup (figure 18). In his will he left money to each order of friars in Cambridge for masses to commemorate him, and money likewise to the Abbess and sisters of Denny for prayers for himself and his parents.

Thus during the early centuries of the College were laid down features of college life that can still be recognised today; the site and buildings, the Master, Tutors, Fellows, undergraduates, college teaching, manuscripts, silver, music and community life. A small foundation adapted itself constantly to changes in the development of the University and the needs of the outside world and was, from the beginning, notable in combining piety towards its origin with a position in the forefront of new University developments.

Figure 18 The Foundress's Cup. The cup belongs to the class of mazers (Latin *murra*): shallow cups made of close-grained wood (especially maple but sometimes walnut or beech). They were often mounted in silver, with an edging and a so-called print in the middle where the grain was weak. The edging might be extended by a deep margin and the whole set on a base. There might also be a cover. This cup had all these features. There are no hallmarks. Similar cups are all dated between 1460 and 1500. At some time the wooden bowl was replaced by silver gilt. The cover (assuming that the original wooden one had been replaced by silver) was no doubt sent to King Charles at the time of the Civil Wars, the cup itself being retained because of its supposed association with the Foundress. The print is now missing.

The main inscription, '*Sayn denes that es me dere for hes lof drenk and mak gud cher*' [Saint Denys who is dear to me – in praise of him, drink and make good cheer] is in northern English, Sokburn coming from York Diocese. It is not known why St Denys is named on the cup. (The feast of St Denys (or the day after, i.e. 10 October) is mentioned in the early statutes but this is simply because it was the customary way to refer to the start of the University year.) 'VM' (for Valence Mary, the original name of the College), in roughly engraved letters, must have been added after the gift was made.

Probably given by Richard Sockborn, Fellow 1470, Vicar of Soham (d. 1502). It is described in an inventory after 1497 as 'a silver murra with writing around it, "God help at ned", and with a wooden cover having a ball at the top'.

Early benefactions

In order to survive and develop its role as an expanding college in the University, Pembroke needed, and successfully attracted, benefactions from inside and outside its membership.

Marie de St Pol's gift of the three advowsons with their appropriated tithes of Saxthorpe and Tilney in Norfolk and Waresley in Huntingdonshire were the College's first source of income and together brought in just over one hundred pounds. Saxthorpe had been part of the Foundress's dowry. It should be borne in mind that the original endowments of these appropriated churches were often considered to be well in excess of the needs of the parish priest. It was not, therefore, considered an abuse to appropriate the tithes to academic uses. The College still has a share in the appointment of the clergy of its parishes today. In addition, the Foundress acquired a farm at Burwell, which was eventually conveyed through trustees

Figure 19 A Decree for the Obit of King Henry VI. Wherein the College expresses its thankfulness to that most pious Prince for his singular bounty to them, 20 May 1448. The letter, inscribed 'Dieu et mon Droit', was apparently intended for presentation but never sent. The College, 'humbly, like the widow in the Gospel offers the mites (hec minuta) which follow', promising masses and prayers for Henry VI and Queen Margaret (as also for the King's parents, Henry V and Queen Catherine), during the remainder of his reign and after his death. (College Archives, College Box A19.)

to the College, and rent charges from property in Repton in Derbyshire (exchanged for rents in Gransden) and Whissendine in Rutland. By her will she left the College one hundred marks and various relics and ornaments, none of which survives.

Henry VI is known as the College's second Founder, for conferring upon it English property of alien – that is, French – priories which had been sequestered during the French Wars of King Henry V. This use of alien priory lands was part of his general educational patronage, in which he was encouraged by John Langton and John Somerset, both from Pembroke, who were high in his service (see above, p. 24). The College thus received Linton Priory, with its impropriate rectory (though not the advowson) and a cell at Isleham, whose chapel is now Isleham Barn, an ancient monument. These, with related lands, were former possessions of the Cistercians of St Jacut of the Isle (Côtes-du-Nord). The College also obtained the rectory and advowson of Soham, formerly belonging to the Cistercian Abbey of le Pin (Vienne).

William Lyndewode, canon lawyer, Bishop of St David's and a colleague of Langton and Somerset, founded, with Robert Pyke a chest

Figure 20 Richard Foxe (1448–1528). Related to the portrait of Foxe at Corpus Christi College, Oxford, of which numerous versions exist.

(Lyndewode and Pyke's Fund, still in existence) from which money could be lent to Fellows in exchange for a pledge, usually a book.

Laurence Booth's work in the early College has been mentioned above. He was also a major benefactor: indeed, few if any have done more for the College. His major gifts to the old Chapel have been described (p. 18); the music there was enhanced; the garden was set with saffron. He gave to Pembroke all those houses, known as 'The Island', situated between the College and St Botolph's, and he bequeathed the manor and advowson of Orton Waterville in Huntingdonshire. It was Booth who secured for the College the perpetual lease of St Thomas's Hostel in 1451 (p. 14) and on the accession of Edward IV he took care to secure for the College Henry VI's gifts of Soham, Linton and Isleham, which might otherwise have been lost. As has been noted, it was in Booth's time that the Library was put in above the Hall. Other grand Masters gave and did less: Richard Foxe, Bishop of Winchester and Master 1506–1518 (figure 20), made gifts of money and chantries but, like Rotherham, founded his own institution, Corpus Christi College, Oxford.

Figure 21 *Gospels*

In Latin, dating from about 1020. The beginning of each gospel has a display page with illuminated text initial and, facing it, an evangelist portrait, the two leaves being intended to be viewed as one. These openings were executed by different artists and are in some cases unfinished. This one shows Matthew.

The book belonged to a certain Andrew Jenour in the seventeenth century. He was not, apparently, a member of Pembroke but may have been the Fellow Commoner of that name who matriculated from Queens' College in 1659. How the book came to Pembroke is not known. (Pembroke College MS 301.)

Figure 22 *New Testament* (the 'Bury Gospels'). This splendid copy of the New Testament in Latin was written in the first half of the twelfth century, possibly at Bury St Edmunds, and given to that Abbey by its sacrist, Reginald of Denham, who held office in the early fourteenth century. The book contains the Gospels, Acts, Catholic Epistles, Pauline Epistles and Apocalypse (Revelation).

The page above is one of twelve with which the book begins, containing forty illustrations from the Gospels. Some of these show rarely depicted episodes, such as the middle panel here depicting the parable of the Guest without a Wedding Garment. The other panels show Christ threatened with stoning (top) and the Entry into Jerusalem (bottom). These leaves have been trimmed down at the edges, suggesting that they originally came from another book.

The main text includes historiated initials (i.e. with a picture) of high quality, though without the full-page frontispieces of the Evangelists found in very early Gospel Books.

This book is generally identified with the 'Novum Testamentum MS. in folio' recorded by Matthew Wren as the gift to the College of his friend and chaplain Edmund Boldero, Fellow, 1630–44, afterwards Master of Jesus College. (Pembroke College MS. 120.)

Other lands came from Edward Storey, Bishop of Chichester, who also gave a set of vestments of white satin for the chapel. William Atkinson, an original Fellow of Jesus College gave the College lands, as did Gerard Skipwith and his brother Nicholas. The Booth family gave property in London, and the end of the fifteenth century was a time of increasing endowments and gifts.

From the earliest period, the most frequent gifts to the College were of books, a large number of which are still owned by the College. One of the earliest recorded gifts came from William Stybard, Fellow in 1358–9, including probably MS. 165, *Liber Sextus Decretalium*, a canon law text. A much older volume, given by John Sudbury, Master 1428,

Figure 23 Gospel lectionary (the 'Hereford Gospels'). A Gospel lectionary in Latin, from the mid-eleventh century, containing extracts from the Gospels to be read during the liturgy (i.e. not the complete text).

The extracts from each Gospel begin with a large ornamental initial, preceded by a full-page portrait of the evangelist in gold and colour, seated against a curtained ground. The intensity of the colours and the lively impression of movement are remarkable. The page above shows Luke, who has a quill stuck behind his ear and bends over an open book.

Written in England, the Gospels were at Hereford at least in the late eleventh century, since they contain a description in a hand of that date of the boundaries of the see drawn up by Athelstan, Bishop of Hereford *c.* 1013–56, added in Old English on a blank leaf. Given by William Mundy, elected Fellow in 1722. (Pembroke College MS. 302.)

is a copy of Ezekiel (MS. 147), a fine example of a twelfth-century glossed biblical manuscript, still in its original binding.

In addition to those given by the Foundress, altar furnishings and vestments were given later by John Fewterer (Fellow 1515), who entered the Abbey of Syon, eventually becoming fifth Confessor General. Fewterer was one of several Fellows to be associated with Syon. An earlier Confessor General had been Thomas Westhaugh (Fellow, 1436) donor of twelve books, which all survive. The abbey had come to attract men from the universities; it is tempting to wonder whether Pembroke's association with Denny Abbey meant that its Fellows were drawn to this celebrated convent of learned men and women. All this was to change at the Reformation, but the College would continue to expand, and attract benefactions.

Jayne Ringrose

3 THE SIXTEENTH CENTURY

This century saw in Pembroke its first great poet, Edmund Spenser, and its first scientist, the naturalist William Turner. Its history in this period, however, is dominated not by these but by a long succession of great churchmen, many of whom served as Master. The remarkable story of the Pembroke bishops continued into the first part of the seventeenth century and it is appropriate here to trespass onto the territory of the following chapter and deal with them all in a single narrative. In terms of its buildings, the College remained in the sixteenth century essentially as it had been since the time of the Foundress.

Pembroke bishops

When in 1655 Thomas Fuller came to tell of Pembroke in his *History of the University of Cambridge*, he did not stint his words. 'Let Pembroke Hall be compared with any foundation in Europe, not exceeding it in bigness, time and number of Members, and it will acquit it self not conquered in all learned and liberal capacities.' A particular source of this enthusiasm was the twenty-two bishops that he listed for the College over its 300-year history, far in excess of what any other House had produced, such as the five he noted from Peterhouse or the six from Caius. Fuller was also impressed by the almost unbroken succession of Pembroke Masters over the previous hundred years who had, often at the same time, been bishop: 'Unparallel'd in any English Foundation.'

Pembroke, perhaps uniquely in Cambridge, had early preferred men of influence from outside its walls as Masters. A papal bull had been obtained to allow this in 1450. For many generations such men were likely to be bishops. If in Laurence Booth Pembroke had the first head of house to become, in 1476, also Archbishop in the English church, to elect as next Master in 1480 Thomas Rotherham, his successor as Archbishop of York and still Chancellor of England, was to put Pembroke on the map in a way that other Colleges would increasingly attempt to emulate with grandees of their own.

Two more Pembroke Masters were to be also bishops before the Reformation threatened to turn episcopacy upside down. Roger Leyburn, one-time Fellow, was Bishop of Carlisle when elected in 1505. His patron Richard Foxe (p. 29) had, since his days in exile with Henry Tudor, become so grand as to sweep through bishoprics at Exeter, Bath and Wells, Durham, and finally the plum of Winchester, before in 1507 taking on Pembroke too. As an executor of the will of Henry VII, he was to devise the first glazed windows in King's new Chapel. But his interest, when not at the court of Henry VIII where, until Wolsey, he was among the most influential of ministers, was to be occupied by the founding of Corpus, Oxford.

Foxe was a friend of the finest scholar in Europe, Erasmus, who in 1511 had come to Cambridge to lecture in the rediscovered language of the New Testament, Greek. His New Testament of 1516, the first ever printed Greek text, set alight the study of scripture, which was at the heart of the pending Reformation. His assistant at Cambridge was Thomas Lupset of Pembroke. 'Lupset esteems himself born anew by our aid,' Erasmus wrote to Sir Thomas More in 1515, 'and simply saved from perdition. The masters make every exertion to drag the young man back to their treadmill; for on the very first day he had thrown away their sophistical books and bought Greek.' Another Pembroke convert to Greek, George Stafford, Fellow from 1515, was to be widely remembered for his lectures on St Paul: 'He seemed of a dead man to make him alive again and ... to set him forth in his native colours.' Into this ferment of scholarship, from Newcastle to Pembroke, came Nicholas Ridley, in 1518 probably aged fifteen.

Ridley became an outstanding scholar in both Greek and Latin and in his final testament recalled Pembroke Hall affectionately 'to be studious, well learned, and a great setter forth of Christ's gospel ... In thy orchard (the walls, buts and trees, if they could speak, would bear me witness) I learned, without book, almost all St Paul's epistles, yea, and I ween all the canonical epistles, save only the book of Revelation' – doubtless in Greek. By the mid 1520s Lutheran views, seeping from Germany into East Anglia, were alarming the authorities at Cambridge, Stafford and John Rogers being among four Fellows of Pembroke suspected of heresy. Ridley is not known to have yet been sympathetic to such views, though his skill in debate was becoming renowned. Elected Fellow in 1524, he returned in 1530 after five years' study on the continent to be Junior, then Senior Treasurer of the College, apparently putting its finances on a sound basis. His patient teaching of Greek was remembered by a Pembroke student, the future botanist, William Turner (see p.50), as well as their competing together at archery and handball.

By the time Ridley became chaplain to Archbishop Cranmer in

Figure 24 Nicholas Ridley. Engraving by P. van Gunst; plate to Larrey's *Histoire de l'Angleterre* (1697).

Figure 25 Ridley's Chair. A sixteenth-century board-seated chair, of ash, with turned posts and rails and with the spaces in the back, below the elbow rails and below the front rail filled with turned spindles. Such board-seated turned chairs were made for ceremonial purposes and represent one of the high points of the furniture-maker's craft at the time: few survive. Bequeathed to Pembroke in 1928 by the widow of W. H. Ridley.

1537 his religious views had changed and with them the shape of his career. After nineteen years in Cambridge Ridley moved to the world of high politics, noticed soon by Henry VIII as one of his chaplains. Pembroke seized the opportunity in 1540 to elect him Master and by 1547, on Henry's death, Ridley was at the forefront of the new protestant thinking as Bishop of Rochester. His new position, elevated further as Bishop of London in 1550, brought him occasionally to Cambridge, as did his duties as Master: purging the University of superstition, sorting out the legal tangles at the College living of Soham, ordaining divinity students in the College chapel.

In July 1553 the young King, Edward VI, died, bequeathing the crown to protestant Lady Jane Grey. Ten days later Ridley in a London sermon declared Catholic Mary a bastard and therefore incapable of succeeding to the throne. Within four days he was in the Tower. By 1554 he was no longer Master, his successor, John

Figure 26 John Bradford. Detail from the College's portrait, which is based on the engraving in *Heroologia Anglicanum* (1620).

Young, taking part in the Oxford disputations and visiting him in prison there to persuade him to recant. In February 1555 John Rogers of Pembroke, friend of Tyndale and editor of the English Bible known as *Matthew's*, was first to be burned at Smithfield. In July John Bradford, the former soldier whom Ridley had recruited to Pembroke as Fellow in 1549, was also put to the stake at Smithfield, remembered as well for his earlier words before an execution of criminals: 'But for the grace of God there goes John Bradford' – the origin of the English phrase. To burn a bishop was a harder matter. But on 16 October Ridley and Bishop Latimer were brought to their burning outside the walls of Oxford, Ridley with considerable agony as Latimer famously called out: 'Be of good comfort, Master Ridley, and play the man; we shall this day by God's grace light such a candle in England, as I trust shall never be put out.'

The candle was by many carried abroad during Mary's five years as Queen, among them by Edmund Grindall. 'He is a Pembroke Hall man,' Gabriel Harvey said of him, 'ergo, a good scholar'. As President under Ridley, Grindall had been responsible for the College in the Master's absence. In exile in Germany he organised what was to become one of the most influential books in English identity – Foxe's *Book of Martyrs*. On Elizabeth's accession Grindall returned to be Bishop of London, at the same time persuaded by Pembroke to be Master in place of Young. Grindall, with Bradford, had much favoured the continental reformer Martin Bucer, Regius Professor briefly at Cambridge. (Bucer died in Cambridge and was buried at Great St Mary's. Another one-time Pembroke Fellow, John Christopherson, appointed by Mary to be Bishop of Chichester, busied himself in the burning of Bucer's disinterred bones outside the University Church.) But other views were emerging in what is loosely called 'puritanism'. In 1575 Grindall moved as Archbishop from York to Canterbury, having resigned the mastership to his former chaplain Matthew Hutton in 1562. Pembroke continued to turn to Grindall for advice over two subsequent mastership elections but in 1577 he found himself in virtual imprisonment by the Queen over 'puritan prophesyings', which he refused to suppress. When the next Master was needed, the College asked advice of Elizabeth's favourite, the Earl of Leicester, instead.

Grindall was not alone in showing discretion towards Calvinistic puritanism in the English Church. Hutton, his successor as Master until made Dean of York in 1567, came to a similar stance. But such views, coupled with Hutton's independence of spirit, did not favour him for further promotion for the next twenty-one years (he was to be remarkably placed in the Reformation pantheon as combining 'the understanding of Bucer with the memory of Peter Martyr and the vigour of Calvin'). But in 1589 he became Bishop of Durham and six years later Archbishop of York. His successor, as both Master of Pembroke and Regius Professor, was John Whitgift, who was marked out for far more rapid elevation, leaving his old College within three months to be Master of Trinity. By 1577 he was Bishop of Worcester and in 1583 was appointed Archbishop of Canterbury after Grindall. When Hutton went to York in 1595 both Archbishops were former Pembroke Masters.

Figure 27 Edmund Grindall. The College's portrait is one of several similar versions, all probably dating from the late sixteenth century.

Whitgift, who had matriculated in Pembroke in 1550 when Ridley was still Master, had been tutored by John Bradford. On his election as Master the Fellows expressed their thanks that the tradition of Ridley was in safe hands; the martyred bishop was already a legend and was long to remain part of Pembroke's self-understanding. If more of the administrator and less subtle in religion than his patron Grindall, Whitgift stood with firmness for a moderate Calvinism in a Church increasingly disturbed by extremes. In the controversies over predestination and election, Bradford had refused to pinpoint the 'saved' and in this he was followed by Whitgift. So too Lancelot

Andrewes, at Pembroke from 1571, though opposed in many ways to Whitgift's position, preached that 'we are not anxiously to enquire and search out God's secret will touching reprobation or election'. This continuity of moderation among overlapping Pembroke theologians in such a divisive issue has been viewed sufficiently remarkable as to be dubbed 'the Pembroke contribution to English theology'.

Grindall's influence lived on when another of his chaplains, John Young, succeeded Whitgift as Master in 1567. He had managed to keep his fellowship through the mastership of his namesake under Mary but when made Bishop of Rochester in 1578 he finally left the College. He was to be celebrated as the Argus-eyed 'Roffy' by Edmund Spenser who had been part of the notable literary intake at Pembroke during Young's mastership.

William Fulke, his successor at Pembroke, was temporarily to break the succession of episcopal Masters. Not nominated by the disgraced Grindall, he was in his day as famous as many of them through the asperity of his controversial pamphlets against Rome. He had earlier published a *Book of Meteors* (1563), which ran to five editions over the next hundred years and prompted Fuller to opine that 'afterwards his endeavours ascended from the middle region of the aire, to the higher heavens, when he became a pious and solid divine'. But with no mitre he was Master till death in 1589.

Greek was still being promoted in these years. Grindall had sponsored a Greek lectureship in the College and had helped the Master, John Young, secure the benefaction in 1571 of seven Greek scholarships from Thomas Watts, whose widow Young married. The candidates had, for a starter, to be 'such as have Learned ye Latin & Greek Grammars & The Catechisme of Mr John Calvin in Greeke'. Over the subsequent century five of these Watts scholars were to become bishops: Thomas Dove at Peterborough, Theophilus Field at Llandaff and briefly at Hereford, Samuel Puleyn Archbishop of Tuam, Matthew Wren at Norwich and Ely, and Lancelot Andrewes, who also succeeded Fulke as Master.

Andrewes had the gift of languages such that it was said he learned a new language each year. He also loved teaching and after pipping Dove at the fellowship competition of 1576 was to become renowned among town and gown for his College catechetical lectures, Calvinist in tone, of which the careful notes taken by a pupil survive in the College library. Later his shrewd catholic piety, which drew on the early Fathers and emphasised the visible sacramental character of Christian faith, afforded an alternative to the puritan pattern that had been influential in Pembroke under Fulke as in the church at large.

In 1589 at the age of 34 Andrewes was elected Master. Already, however, he was being called away as a preacher, though he was regularly present at the annual Audit and must have delighted at the

Figure 28 William Fulke (1538–1589). Frontispiece to his *New Testament* (1633).

large collection of medieval manuscripts originating from the Abbey at Bury St Edmunds which came to Pembroke from William Smart in 1598. As a scholar, and now Dean of Westminster, he was summoned to the Hampton Court Conference of 1604 convened by the new King, James, to bring together a small band representative of presbyterians and churchmen. Among these latter from Pembroke were Dove of Peterborough and John Bridges soon to be Bishop of Oxford; Archbishop Whitgift was too close to death to come, Hutton too far away and old, though characteristically he sent his views, 'that neither the Papists obtain their hoped toleration, nor the Puritans their phantastical platform of their Reformation'.

The one positive outcome of the Conference was the decision to produce an Authorised Version of the Bible. Andrewes, the Hebraist, chaired the panel for Genesis to II Kings and three other Pembroke divines were also translators, including Andrewes' brother Roger, later Master of Jesus. But Pembroke may be said to have helped also prepare the way for this literary achievement. One of the versions by which the King ordered them to be guided was *Matthew's*, which the 'proto-martyr' Rogers had edited (and of which Andrewes' copy is now in the College library); and the ground rules for the style and language owe much to Fulke's pamphlet warfare against the 'affected novelties of terms such as neither English nor Christian ears had ever heard in the English tongue', used in the Roman Catholic attempt at an English New Testament in 1582.

Andrewes the preacher was also shaping the English language as the favourite for court sermons on the important ecclesiastical and political anniversaries. His elaborate but tightly crafted expounding of doctrine came to be ranked by T. S. Eliot 'with the finest English prose of the time, of any time', a tribute Eliot was to flesh out by directly quoting Andrewes' words from the Christmas sermon of 1622 in the opening of his *Journey of the Magi*: 'A cold comming they had of it, at this time of the yeare; just, the worst time of the yeare, to take a journey, and specially a long journey, in. The waies deep, the weather sharp, the daies short, the sunn farthest off *in solstitio brumali*, the very dead of *Winter*.' In an age of eminent preaching Andrewes was not without rivals – Ralph Brownrigg, Fellow of Pembroke and Bishop of Exeter 1642–59, is reckoned one of the finest of the Calvinist metaphysical preachers. But others doubtless came to sympathise with Nicholas Felton, later Master of the College and favoured by Andrewes, who was said to have 'indeavoured in vain in his Sermon to assimilate his style, and therefore said merrily of himself; I had almost marr'd my own natural Trot by endeavouring to imitate his artificial Amble'.

Figure 29 Lancelot Andrewes. By Joseph Boxhorne. A Latin inscription on the back of the panel relates that the painting was 'Done by Boxhorne of the Hague after the original likeness which without the Bishop's knowledge his secretary Samuel Wright (being skilled alike with pen and brush) painted at lunchtime unobserved'. Boxhorne came to London in 1670 and probably did the painting after that date, long after Andrewes' death in 1626.

Andrewes' enduring influence however lies in his prayers. After his death in 1626, Richard Drake, Fellow of the College, published in 1648 *A Manual of the Private Devotions and Meditations* of Andrewes, drawn from a small manuscript volume of 170 pages now in the College library, which his friend Samuel Wright had copied when secretary to the Bishop. (Another, different copy exists at St John's College, Oxford.) Andrewes liked to say his prayers to God in the best language, Latin, and then to turn them into the language of the New Testament, Greek, and since the prayers were redolent with scripture, Hebrew too. They were his private prayers, *Preces Privatae*, but, in a variety of English translations since Drake, their gentle, penitential, grateful, comprehensive tone has nourished prayer

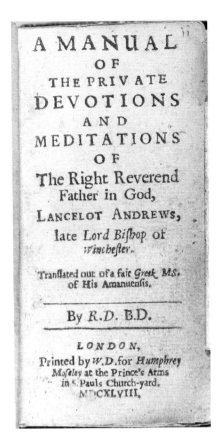

Figure 30 *A Manual of the Private Devotions and Meditations of the Right Rev. Father in God, Lancelot Andrewes* (London 1648). The first published translation, by R. D(rake), of Andrewes' *Private Devotions*, of which part of the manuscript is reproduced right.

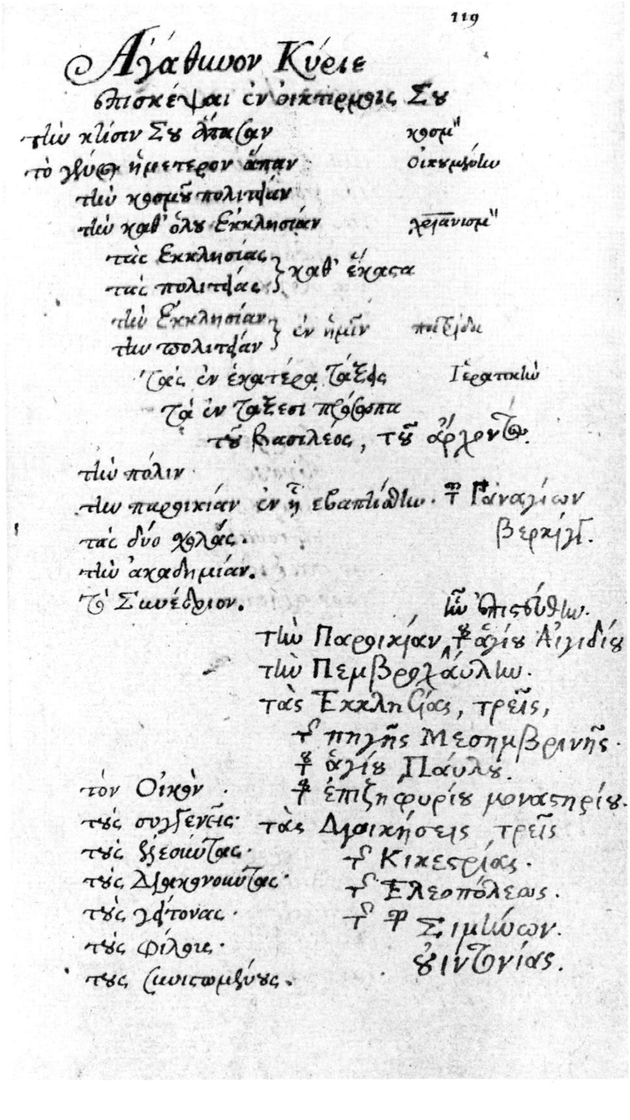

Figure 31 Manuscript of Andrewes' *Private Devotions*. Largely in Greek, two hands are evident, of which the smaller, neater is that of Andrewes' amanuensis, Samuel Wright, on whose sketch of Andrewes the portrait reproduced in figure 29 was based. In another hand are interpolated Andrewes' more personal intercessions, taken from another manuscript, including, as here, a reference to Pembroke.

worldwide. Henry Seite, a publisher of Andrewes in the 1630s, summed up his life as 'Dr Andrews in the School, Bishop Andrews in the pulpit, Saint Andrews in the Closet'. A remembrance of Lancelot Andrewes occurs in the 1980 calendar of the Church of England on 25 September, the nearest Pembroke has come to having a canonised saint yet.

Inevitably Andrewes had been pressed to promotion: Bishop of Chichester in 1605, Ely 1609, and when Canterbury eluded him, Winchester in 1618 (hence the graceful tomb and effigy in Southwark Cathedral, then part of his diocese). He resigned the mastership when consecrated to Chichester but continued influential in College. His successor, Samuel Harsnett, sharing something of Andrewes' views, had been appointed to the living of Chigwell; they had coincided as Fellows. In 1610 he followed Andrewes as Bishop of Chichester but unlike Andrewes resided in his diocese rather than at court and did not resign as Master. A group of Fellows, led by Matthew Wren, soon started to complain, not least at his deputies. Wren and Harsnett matched each other in language, Wren calling Harsnett 'so potent, crafty, and violent an adversary', Harsnett one of the Fellows 'a stiffe, saucy clowne' and bidding another to go schoolmastering. Andrewes from Ely could not help intervening. Things came to a head when the Calvinist Brownrigg combined with the catholic Wren to collect 63 complaints to present to the King at Thetford in May 1616 and Harsnett was forced to resign. Yet Harsnett had done well by the College finances, as Vice-Chancellor had defended the independence of the University against the King, and after translation to Norwich was to become, in 1628, Archbishop of York, the fifth Master so to do.

Harsnett's repute however lies in a literary legacy, different again from Andrewes': *A Declaration of Egregious Popish Impostures*, a work vigorously sceptical of demon possession, published by him in 1603. It is the source of much in *King Lear*, not only the devils' names but the origin of many details of Lear's madness and Edgar's simulated possession. There may be echoes too in *Pericles*, *The Tempest* and *Cymbeline*. Harsnett was buried in 1631 at Chigwell where he founded the school, a fine brass depicting him as a bishop of the catholic church wearing the first mitre in an Anglican portrait.

Through the controversy over Harsnett's mastership Andrewes had favoured as his successor Nicholas Felton, Greek lecturer at the College since 1586. Elected in June 1616 he was by December 1617 also Bishop of Bristol, a diocese even further away than Chichester. But when Andrewes moved to Winchester, Felton came to Ely. The College begged the Chancellor to allow him to continue as Master but he resigned before his translation. He and Andrewes died within a fortnight in 1626. 'Buried before, though dying some days after,' wrote Fuller. 'Great was the conformity between them; both scholars, fellows, and masters of Pembroke Hall; both great scholars and

Figure 32 Nicholas Felton (1556–1626). Probably a contemporary portrait, with an inscription dating it 1623.

painful preachers in London for many years, with no less profit to others than credit to themselves; both successively bishops of Ely.'

A Pembroke succession of Bishops of Ely was to occur once more. Matthew Wren, Felton's deputy, although not Master of Pembroke, was from the mastership of Peterhouse made Bishop of Hereford, Norwich, then Ely. He was followed on his death in 1667 by Benjamin Lany who had been the pre-Commonwealth Master in 1630, ejected in 1644, restored in 1660, then rapidly promoted as one-time chaplain to Charles I, via Peterborough and Lincoln to Ely. Lany, though catholic in churchmanship, had been a friend of William Crashaw, a notable puritan divine and father of the future poet Richard (see p. 75), who recorded his delight at Lany's restoration in Pembroke's (old) chapel of the choral service with surpliced choir and an adorned altar.

Lany's predecessor as Master of Pembroke, Jerome Beale, had not been elevated to the bench and Lany himself turned out to be the last Master to be bishop. Indeed, scarcely another bishop is known among Pembroke men until George Pretyman Tomline, tutor to William Pitt, and from 1783 Bishop of Lincoln for 33 years. He it was who, when the first Bishop of Calcutta was looked for in 1814, recommended Thomas Middleton (see p. 121) and so initiated the dis-

Figure 33 Benjamin Lany (1591–1675). Given by his great-nephew Edward Lany (Master, 1707–28).

Figure 34 (opposite) Edmund Spenser. Portrait by Benjamin Wilson, copied by him from an original portrait now lost. Given by William Mason, 1771.

tinguished religious connection of Pembroke with India, most notably in the friend of Gandhi, C.F. Andrews.

On leaving the College Charlie Andrews had been given by the Master, Charles Edward Searle, Drake's 1648 version of Lancelot Andrewes' *Preces*. Perhaps he knew of the bishop's 'Prayer before Sermon':

Lastly, that he would plentifully pour out his blessings upon our Colleges; and (as my speciall duty calls mee) upon the whole Society of Pembrook Hall; that wee gracing our Predecessors who have been always famous in this Church, may follow their industry, considering the end of their conversation.

Brian Watchorn

Edmund Spenser, 'Prince of Poets'

Spenser matriculated as a sizar at Pembroke Hall on 20 May 1569, a 'poor scholar' financially assisted by the estate of the philanthropist Robert Nowell. He had received his early education at the Merchant Taylors' School under the benign, if authoritarian, influence of the celebrated headmaster Richard Mulcaster, and the watchful eyes of the visitor Edmund Grindall, then Bishop of London but formerly Master of Pembroke. His earliest known verse, a set of translations contributed to Jan van der Noot's anti-papal polemic, *A Theatre for Voluptuous Worldlings*, was published during his first months at Pembroke and heralded an intense engagement with the political and religious issues of the age.

At Pembroke Spenser began his lifelong friendship with Gabriel Harvey whose *Letterbook* supplies a unique insight into College life during this period. Brilliant and arrogant in equal measure, Harvey infuriated the other Fellows and provoked unprecedented scenes of academic dissension – as when the Junior Proctor came 'swelling' into the Hall where Harvey was attempting to deliver his Greek lectures and 'commaundith the schollers from the table'. But Harvey was secure in the support of the Master, John Young (formerly Grindall's chaplain), who personally promoted the grace for his MA in 1573 despite opposition from the College. Spenser graduated BA that same year and was still in residence late in 1574 when the University was afflicted by a particularly virulent outbreak of plague. Thereafter, until his appointment as Young's personal secretary in 1578, following the Master's elevation to the see of Rochester, his movements are unknown although the records indicate that he proceeded MA in 1576. Taking full advantage of Young's departure, Harvey's enemies conspired to terminate his fellowship and he moved to Trinity Hall on 18 December 1578. He celebrated the event with Spenser two days later

The firſt Booke of
the Faerie Queene.

Contayning

The Legend of the Knight
of the Red Croſſe,
O R
Of Holineſſe.

LO I the man, whoſe Muſe whylome did maske,
As time her taught, in lowly Shephards weeds,
Am now enforſt a farre vnfitter taske,
For trumpets ſterne to chaunge mine Oaten reeds:
And ſing of Knights and Ladies gentle deeds,
Whoſe praiſes hauing ſlept in ſilence long,
Me, all too meane, the ſacred Muſe areeds
To blazon broade emongſt her learned throng:
Fierce warres and faithfull loues ſhall moralize my ſong.

Helpe then, O holy virgin chiefe of nyne,
Thy weaker Nouice to performe thy will,
Lay forth out of thine euerlaſting ſcryne
The antique rolles, which there lye hidden ſtill,

A 2   Of

Figure 35 Edmund Spenser, *The Faerie Queene*. From the first edition of the first three books (London, 1590).

when they met in London to swap books and plan their future careers.

The following year saw the publication of *The Shepheardes Calender* which served as the manifesto for a sea-change in Tudor poetics and established Spenser as the 'new poet' of the coming generation. Harvey is one of the work's two dedicatees and the scholarly commentary by the mysterious 'E. K.' – sometimes identified as Edward Kirke, another Pembrokian, but probably a collaborative pseudonym for Harvey and Spenser – is eloquent in praise of Harvey's prolific, if stilted, Latin verse. Less opportunistic, and even courageous, is Spenser's support for the now disgraced Grindall, sequestered from his duties as Archbishop of Canterbury owing to his support for what the Queen regarded as unlicensed preaching. While the Elizabethan Church is portrayed as pervasively corrupt, two Pembroke luminaries, 'Algrind' and 'Roffy' – Grindall and Young – shine forth as counter examples, as good shepherds of the reformed faith.

Capitalising upon the enormous success of *The Shepheardes Calender*, Spenser and Harvey published their only joint venture in 1580, a volume of *Familiar Letters* purporting to be the unedited correspondence of 'two University men', but carefully crafted to enhance the reputations of both contributors. In Harvey's case, however, the plan went badly awry. Satirical asides were widely interpreted as personal attacks upon influential public figures while broader academic parodies intensified hostility within the University. Not surprisingly, he failed to gain the Mastership of Trinity Hall in 1585 and migrated to London where he unwisely engaged in controversy with the satirist Thomas Nashe who maliciously represented his relationship with Spenser as manipulative and self-serving.

Spenser had departed for Ireland in 1580 as secretary to the Lord Deputy and finally secured the grant of a sizeable, but embattled, estate in the ill-fated Plantation of Munster. With the publication of the first instalment of *The Faerie Queene* in 1590, he might well have hoped for greater recognition, but his reception by the Queen, though personally gratifying, produced only a small pension, irregularly paid. The volume of aptly entitled *Complaints* which followed in 1591 charted a political and cultural landscape pervaded by hypocrisy, graft and greed, and the mood of depression deepened considerably in *Colin Clouts Come Home Againe* (1595). Only within the private world of the *Amoretti* and *Epithalamion* (1595), which explore the experience of courtship and marriage, does the poet express contentment or satisfaction. By contrast, in the second instalment of *The Faerie Queene* (1596) the heroic ethos is undermined by a corrosive cynicism. Yet, paradoxically, Spenser's poetic powers were at their height, as though morbidly inspired by the decay of his political and cultural vision.

The situation in Ireland worsened daily. Spenser had attempted to alert the authorities to the danger in 'A View of the Present State of

Ireland' (1596), but his warnings had gone unheeded. In 1598 as the combined forces of the O'Neills and the O'Donnells poured southwards from Ulster, he was burned out of his home at Kilcolman and fled to London where he died, apparently in straitened circumstances, on 13 January 1599, leaving *The Faerie Queene* unfinished. Its final fragment, the *Mutabilitie Cantos*, forms an appropriate coda to his epic endeavour in its portrayal of the endless conflict between creativity and decay, idealism and despair. As his friend's posthumous reputation soared, Harvey lingered in disappointed obscurity until 1631, remembered only, if at all, as the one-time companion of the 'Prince of Poets'.

Richard McCabe

To the right worshipfull, my singular good frend,
M. Gabriell Harvey, Doctor
of the Lawes

Harvey, the happy above happiest men
I read: that sitting like a Looker-on
Of this worldes Stage, doest note with critique pen
The sharpe dislikes of each condition:
And as one carelesse of suspistion,
Ne fawnest for the favour of the great:
Ne fearest foolish reprehension
Of faulty men, which daunger to thee threat.
But freely doest, of what thee list, entreat,
Like a great Lord of peerelesse liberty:
Lifting the Good up to high Honours seat,
And the Evill damning evermore to dy.
For Life, and Death is in thy doomefull writing:
So thy renowme lives ever by endighting.

Dublin: this xviii. of July: 1586.

Your devoted frend, during life,
Edmund Spencer.

ΜΩΡΙΑ ΠΑΡΑ ΤΩ ΘΕΩ.

ABRAHAMI ORTELII
THEATRI
ORBIS TERRARVM
PARERGON;
SIVE
VETERIS GEOGRAPHIÆ
TABVLÆ,
Commentarijs Geographicis et Historicis illustratæ.

EDITIO NOVISSIMA,
Tabulis aliquot aucta, et varie emendata atq; innouata,
CVRA ET STVDIO
BALTHASARIS MORETI.

HISTORIÆ OCVLVS
GEOGRAPHIA.

ANTVERPIÆ, EX OFFICINA PLANTINIANA, M. DC. XXIV.

Figure 37 (opposite) A page from William Turner's *Herbal*.

William Turner

'The one is called in Englishe cashes ... I never saw greter plenty of it then I have sene in the hortyard of Pembroke hall in Cambrydge where as I was som tyme a pore felow.' Thus writes William Turner (1510–68), describing in his great *Herbal* the plant that we now call cow parsley (*Anthriscus sylvestris*). His book is the starting point of systematic botany in England; Turner himself was the first major student of natural history in this country. He was one of two great biologists produced by Pembroke in the space of a century or so, the other being Nehemiah Grew (p. 74).

Turner was born in Morpeth, Northumberland, and came up to Pembroke in 1526. There was an established connection at that time between the College and that county. Nicholas Ridley, for example, at school in Newcastle, had entered Pembroke a few years before and became Turner's friend and mentor, teaching him Greek. Turner was elected to a fellowship soon after graduating and remained in Cambridge for the next ten years. Like other of the herbalists at that time he was closely connected with the Reformation. He embraced Ridley's views and was a protagonist of Protestantism throughout his life. The fluctuating fortunes of the Reformers markedly influenced his career. During the reign of Henry VIII his religious writings were banned and he was imprisoned. He came back into favour on Edward VI's accession to the throne and was eventually appointed Dean of Wells. In Mary's reign he was exiled but he returned under Elizabeth, to whom his *Herbal* bears a fulsome dedication.

Turner travelled extensively on the Continent when his religious views excluded him from England. These travels enabled him not only to study the European flora but to meet other students of his subject, notably the great Swiss naturalist, Conrad Gesner.

Turner produced two small early botanical works, *Libellus de re herbaria novus* (1538), which is a list of 144 plants with their synonyms in Greek and English and notes on their medicinal and other uses, and *The names of herbes in Greke, Latin, Englishe, Duche, and Frenche with the commune names that Herbaries and Apotecaries use*, which described much more fully 'in what places of Englande, Germany and Italy the herbes growe and maye be had for laboure and money'. His *Herbal*, published in three parts between 1551 and 1568, is on a very different scale from these modest publications. It deals with many more plants, and describes numerous species that have no medicinal uses. The first scientific records of 238 of our native English plants are to be found there, along with much information about Continental species. We owe to Turner many of our familiar common names of plants: goats-beard, loose-strife, hawkweed and ground pine, for example. The work as a whole far surpasses anything that had been done in England before.

Of Fenegreck.

Fragraria   Strauuberrie

and afterward rede. The leafe is in-
dētid/ꝗ alwayes thre of them grow
together/ꝥ rote is in som place blake
and som place redyſhe.

The vertues of Strawberries.

Strawberies leaues ta
ken in meate/ helpeth
thē that are diſeaſed in
the milt/ ꝗ ſo doth alſo
the inice dronkē wyth
hony. The ſame is good
to be geuen wyth peper for them that
are ſhort winded. Strawberryes
quenche thirſt/ and are good for a
cholerike ſtomack. Ther is a inice
preſſed out of ſtrawberries/whiche
by cōtinuance of tyme encreaſeth in
ſtrēgh/ and that is a preſent remedy
againſt the ſores and wheales of the
face/ꝗ againſt the blodſhotten eyes.
The brothe of the rothe ſwageth the
heate of the liuer/ dronken the mor-
ninge eueninge. Many vſe this herbe
to ioyne together grene woundes/ to
ſtoppe laxes/and iſhewes of women/
to ſtrenghehen the gūmes/ ꝗ to take
away the ſores or wheales of ꝥ mouth/and the ſtinkinge of the ſame. The
frut ſemeth to haue ſom warmenes in it/but the leafe is colde.

Of the Aſhe tree.

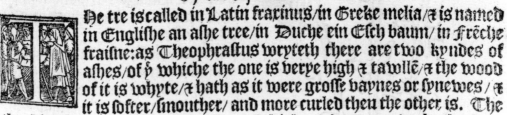

He tre is called in Latin fraxinus/in Greke melia/ꝗ is named
in Engliſhe an aſhe tree/in Duche ein Eſch baum/ in Frēche
fraiſne: as Theophraſtus wryteth there are two kyndes of
aſhes/of ꝥ whiche the one is verye high ꝗ tawllē/ꝗ the wood
of it is whyte/ꝗ hath as it were groſſe vaynes or ſynewes / ꝗ
it is ſofter/ſmouther/ and more curled then the other is. The
other kinde is lower and groweth not ſo highe/and more rowghe/harder/

Turner also studied both birds and fishes. On the former his *Avium praecipuarum* is full of detailed, first-hand accounts of many British species and is the first work to treat birds with anything like a modern scientific approach.

Turner belongs, of course, to the Renaissance. In his work on the English flora he sees his first task as being to relate his observations to what the classical authors had described. His descriptions of plants and birds show him, however, to have been a keen observer, with a deep interest and delight in nature. He helped to inaugurate the scientific approach to living things.

A. V. Grimstone

(Adapted from an article in *PCCS Annual Gazette* **57** (1983).)

Figure 38 Archive boxes in the College Treasury, made 1502.

4 THE SEVENTEENTH CENTURY

Pembroke's history in the seventeenth century was inevitably influenced by the religious and political upheavals that affected the nation at large. From a religious bias towards puritanism it began under Lancelot Andrewes to develop into a stronghold of the High Church party. In the Civil War it was, like most Cambridge colleges, Royalist. Its poets of the time, Richard Crashaw the Catholic mystic among them, were Royalist too. At the outbreak of the war it sent its plate, except for the two medieval cups, to help the King's cause. Benjamin Lany, the Master, was ejected by the Roundheads and Richard Vines 'intruded' in his place. Another Pembroke royalist, Matthew Wren, a key figure in the College in the early part of the century, later Bishop of Ely and associate of Archbishop Laud, suffered prolonged imprisonment for his High Church affiliations. The College chapel, designed by his nephew Christopher Wren, was his thanks-offering for his release. This century saw a Pembroke man, Roger Williams, founding the colony of Rhode Island, and two Americans – John Stone and William Knight – being elected as Fellows. In the seventeenth-century flowering of science Nehemiah Grew played a notable role as one of the first microscopists.

Buildings

IVY COURT

After the first phase of building, in which the original First Court was completed by the end of the fourteenth century, over two hundred years elapsed before any further major development took place. Then, in about 1614 work began on the north (Pembroke Street) side of what we now know as Ivy Court (originally named New Court). The western two-thirds of this range were completed by 1616, the rest was added in 1670, when the land was acquired. It is a two-storied building, with attics and lofts, in a Tudor style, still essentially medieval. The materials are brick with Ketton stone

Figure 39 Engraving from Loggan's *Cantabrigia Illustrata* (c. 1681). This detailed image, notable, like all Loggan's views, for its conscientious accuracy, is valuable in showing many features of the College buildings as they existed up to the 1870s. Old Court appears essentially in its medieval form, apart from the stone facing. The original chapel has not yet been converted into a library and retains its Gothic west window.

54

COLLEGIUM sive AULA PEMBROCHIANA apud Cant.

David Loggan delin: & Sculps: Cum Privil: S.R.M.

16

Figure 40 Ivy Court, north range.

dressings. The Pembroke Street facade, with stone gables over the dormers and five tall brick chimneys, is more imposing than the court side, where the dormers are timber-framed and lack gables. However, Loggan (figure 39) shows that as originally built these dormers were like those on the street side; their present more modest form dates from the 18th or 19th century. The mason for the 1670 work on this range was Robert Grumbold, who built and designed much else in Cambridge and was later to be Wren's master mason at Trinity College library.

The south range of Ivy Court, begun in 1659 and completed in 1661, is known as Hitcham Building, being built with money bequeathed by Sir Robert Hitcham. His arms appear on both sides of the building. Hitcham Building was completed by one mason, John Young, and it is apparently of one build, yet it consists of two stylistically quite distinct sections. The east part follows closely the pattern of the other side of the court, while the west part forms a distinctive and more complex architectural composition (figure 42). Here, firstly, the windows have stone transoms as well as mullions. Secondly, instead of simple stone gables, the three dormers are given prominent stone pediments, the wide central one segmental, the lateral ones triangular. The wide central bay is carried down through the rest of the facade, the central pair of windows at each level being linked by brick panels and those at first-floor level being surmounted by a triangular pediment. All these features announce the first appearance in Pembroke of the Classical style, which was soon to find full expression in Wren's chapel. The explanation of the greater distinction of this part of the range is perhaps that it was intended for the Master's use. The large room on the first floor (where

Thomas Gray and William Pitt were to live) has at its west end a doorway that would have led to the Lodge.

The design of the whole south range of Ivy Court is attributed to Peter Mills, who came from London 'to lay out the plot'. Mills, originally a bricklayer, had become a surveyor and architect and, after the Great Fire, was to be one of the four surveyors appointed by the City to supervise the rebuilding of London. He was working elsewhere in East Anglia at about the same time as he was engaged on Hitcham Building, designing Thorpe Hall, near Peterborough (1654–6) and Wisbech Castle (*c.* 1658).

The gables throughout Ivy Court bear characteristic finials, consisting of a ball set on a square support. The pattern of these ball finials was adopted by both Waterhouse (e.g. on the Library) and by Caröe on Pitt Building.

Figure 41 Sir Robert Hitcham. Drawing after the engraving in Loder's *History of Framlingham.* Hitcham was a major benefactor. He was a pensioner at the college in 1587 and had a distinguished legal career. In 1636, wishing to benefit the College, he bought the castle, manor and advowson of Framlingham in Suffolk and left them in his will to Pembroke, at the same time making the College trustees for various other charitable bequests. The money thus received was used both for Hitcham Building and for the cloisters (figure 107) with rooms above, built to link Wren's Chapel to Old Court.

Figure 42 Ivy Court, western end of the south range.

Matthew Wren's Library Benefactors Book

As part of a programme to repair and improve the College Library, Wren produced a Library Benefactors Book in his own hand. He begins with a summary of the history of the Library from the earliest period and proceeds to a list of Library benefactors, carried down to his own day. In all this he makes use of material he had found in the College Archives. His discoveries are set out as splendidly as possible, with heraldry where appropriate. At the beginning of the book were drawn two laurel trees, one with yellow autumn leaves, each bearing the name of a deceased benefactor, the other with green leaves, for the names of living benefactors. The intention was clear: there was plenty of room in the book to record further benefactors, ample foliage to receive new names.

Figure 43

MATTHEW WREN AND THE CHAPEL

The story of how Pembroke came to have Christopher Wren's first completed building and the first chapel wholly in the Classical style of any Oxford or Cambridge college must necessarily begin with some account of Matthew Wren (1585–1667), uncle of the architect and an outstanding figure in Pembroke in the early part of the seventeenth century.

Matthew Wren

Of humble birth, Matthew Wren was educated at Merchant Taylors' School and brought to Pembroke at the age of sixteen by the Master, Lancelot Andrewes. He became a Fellow in 1605. 'His habits throughout life were those of a hardy scholar, up at five and seldom in bed till eleven', and he was also an efficient administrator, a combination of qualities that led to his swift rise within Pembroke. He is to be remembered first for his work on the history of the College. Combining antiquarian interests with a love of order, he busied himself in the College Archives, making or annotating lists of documents, and transcribing some of them. His records are important in that they sometimes provide information from documents now lost. Wren's reforming zeal was not restricted to the College archives. By 1615 he had not only secured his position in Pembroke but had gained a foothold at Court, having impressed King James at an academic disputation on whether dogs could make syllogisms. In 1616 the king's favour was vital to Wren when he engineered the resignation of Andrewes' successor as Master, the much-absent Bishop of Chichester, Samuel Harsnett. In the aftermath Wren organized the election to the Mastership of another Fellow, his friend Nicholas Felton (see p. 42), who appointed Wren President (i.e. Vice-Master), an important office at a time when the Master was often absent for long periods. When in 1621 Wren was also made Bursar his two positions effectively gave him disciplinary and financial control over the College.

In 1621 James appointed Wren as chaplain to his son, Charles, Prince of Wales, whom Wren two years later accompanied on a lengthy expedition to Spain. On his return Wren was installed as prebendary of Winchester and had bestowed upon him the wealthy rectory of Bingham in Nottinghamshire, at which point he resigned his Fellowship at Pembroke. His links with the Prince of Wales continued to prove fruitful, for in 1625, Charles, now king, installed Wren as Master of Peterhouse. There he was responsible for the building of the chapel, for which he raised funds, and made the college a focus for high-church practices.

Wren was made Bishop of Hereford in 1634 and resigned the Mastership of Peterhouse shortly afterwards. He was now to become

Wren's portrait

Who could have thought that men would execrate
    That gentle grave young visage? Eighteen years
    A prisoner to their unforgiving fears,
    He walk'd the equator's length on Tower gate.[1]
    Our chapel, dower'd with a fair estate,
    First sample of his nephew's mighty skill,
    Its altar-gear, and every cushion, still
    His late-won liberty commemorate.

    His tomb beneath the chancel he prepared;
    And when the mitred antiquary died,
    Cambridge two days around the body fared,
    Then bore with pomp here to his early nurse,
    And Dugdale marshall'd all by rule of pride,
And Pearson made oration o'er the scutcheon'd hearse.

from A. J. Mason: *Pembroke Sonnets*

Arthur James Mason (1851–1928; Master 1903–12) came to Pembroke as Master via Trinity and then Jesus College. His munificence enabled the bridge (p. 131) to be built; his *Pembroke Sonnets*, used throughout this book, reveal his deep affection for the College.

1 Wren took his daily exercise while in the Tower on the leads of the roof. This was his own computation.

---

one of the most powerful and, indeed, notorious of bishops, playing a significant role in the reforms carried out within the Church of England by Charles I and William Laud, Archbishop of Canterbury. Wren's stay at Hereford was brief, for next year he was moved to Norwich. There, in a large and difficult diocese, he enforced Laudian measures with unbending ferocity and evoked a puritan reaction no less fierce: he was the subject of bitter pamphlet attacks and became the most hated churchman after Archbishop Laud himself. In 1638 Wren was again translated, now to Ely. His time there was less controversial but his tussle with the Puritans at Norwich had earned their unforgiving enmity and when Parliament was recalled in 1640 Wren was one of the chief targets for retribution. The Commons eventually decided that he should be imprisoned until further order and he remained in the Tower of London throughout the Interregnum, eighteen years in all. Initially he was able to live there with his wife, but after her death in 1646 remained there alone, spending his time in study and writing.

While in the Tower Wren vowed that, if he were released, he would devote part of his fortune to some holy purpose. The holy purpose he decided on when, in 1659, an old man of 75, he was even-

tually set free, was the gift of a new chapel to his first College,
Pembroke. Restored as Bishop of Ely in 1660, Wren came to conse-
crate the chapel in 1665. He died two years later. He was quite clear
that the new Chapel was to be his burial place. In his will he wrote:

'*Now* of this New Chappell haveing purposely caused the East end
to be soe raysed, as that under the holy table there is a Vault
strongly inclosed, *My Will* is that (If God soe please) it shalbe for
my owne Sepulture, and for ye interring of the succeeding *Masters*
of the said College if they shall have a minde thereto ...'

He was buried there, as he had intended, on 11 May 1667.

The Chapel

In 1662, when Christopher Wren was invited to design the new chapel,
he was Savilian Professor of Astronomy at Oxford and had never
before designed a building. Wren was, however, perhaps the greatest
intellect of his age and the range of his interests was extraordinarily
wide. He had interested himself in biology as well as astronomy and
mathematics and his drawings of biological specimens reveal his beautiful draughtsmanship and keen aesthetic sense. At all events, he was
seemingly able to turn without difficulty from science to architecture.
Wren's other early building was the Sheldonian Theatre at Oxford, on
which he began work early in 1663. The design is thus more or less contemporary with that of the College Chapel but because of its greater
size and complexity the Sheldonian was not completed until 1669.

Although it has never been seriously questioned that Wren designed
the Chapel, only in 1994 was documentary evidence discovered con-
necting him with the building. This took the form of a set of notes,
found in the College Archives, in Wren's hand, dealing with quanti-
ties, prices, carriage and design of the black and white marble floor.

The College chapel was the earliest purely classical building in
Cambridge. In its great elegance, its assured handling of the classical
style and its complete consistency, inside and out, it must have made
an immense impact in Cambridge. As originally built, it was even
simpler than it now appears, for the present east end was added in
the nineteenth century (see p. 116). Externally it is the west front,
towards the street, that is most imposing (figure 47). Here there is a
large central window and two lateral niches, the three bays so formed
being separated by four pilasters with Corinthian capitals. The
facade is surmounted by a pediment filled with a carved cartouche
draped with garlands. Above the pediment is a hexagonal lantern
and at the four corners of the building are flaming urns carved in
stone. The design has been related to one from Serlio (figure 46).

Figure 47 (opposite) Chapel, west front. Compare with figure 46.

The most remarkable feature of the interior is the ceiling, which gives an almost Baroque flavour. The central part is deeply coved to a depth of five feet, creating the illusionistic effect of a dome. Apart from formal borders, the rich decoration is entirely of foliage and flowers. The ceiling, white and flooded with light from the great windows, floats above the interior, contrasting strongly with the dark panelling below. It is tempting to read this in allegorical terms: the dark world below represents our earthly habitation, the ceiling symbolises Heaven, represented in the flowers and foliage of the plaster-work as a Celestial Garden. Such an interpretation is reinforced by the carving on the panelling: between each alternate bay is an elaborate cartouche with a grotesque mask leering from the bottom, reminding us where we are, and a winged cherub at its top, to take our soul where it should go (figure 50).

It is not known who the plasterers were who worked in the Chapel. The virtuosic quality and complexity of the work is comparable to that done twenty-five years later in the Old Library by Henry Doogood, and he may have been responsible.

Figure 46 Plate from Sebastiano Serlio, *Architettura*. Serlio's manual, published in Venice and Paris from 1537, was the first illustrated architectural treatise in the modern sense and was an essential piece of equipment for the seventeenth-century architect. Christopher Wren's sale included a Venetian edition contemporary with the beginning of work on Pembroke Chapel. The street facade of the Chapel is close to Serlio's elevation of 'the temple by the river at Tivoli'. However, in Serlio's design there is a central entrance, not present in the Chapel.

Figure 48 (opposite) Chapel interior looking west. Apart from the column at left and the arrangement of the stalls, this view has scarcely altered since the Chapel was built.

Figure 49 (right) The elegant hexagonal cupola or lantern is identical to that shown in Loggan's engraving (p. 54) and no doubt in its original form. It has been seen as a precursor of Wren's London church steeples.

Figure 50 (far right) Cartouche from the carving on the panelling.

Figure 51 (below) Chapel model, contemporary with the building and designed to show constructional features. It probably originally had a removable roof. Precise details of the roof trusses are shown, as well as much external detail. Wren made use of such models throughout his career as architect: this is probably the first.

Wall drawings in the Thomas Gray Room (I staircase)

Typically, a seventeenth-century building would not be designed in full detail, by an architect, from the beginning. Decorative details, such as stone carvings, plaster-work and woodwork would be worked out as the job progressed between work-men, architect and patron. These draw-ings, uncovered during renovations in 1965, give a rare glimpse of this process in action.

The Thomas Gray Room (as it is now called) on I staircase in the then newly built Hitcham Building, was apparently used as the construction office for the Chapel. It had plastered walls awaiting panelling and these drawings were made on them. One is a full-size rendering of the cartouche and garlands on the west pediment of the Chapel, the other a full-size rendering of one of the flaming urns on the corners of the building.

The drawings were presumably made either by the mason, as a proposal, or by Wren himself, as instruction, or possibly by both, *inter se disputando*. The drawings show evidence of more than one hand and were followed in some particulars but not in others. The hand that outlines the urn is confident and thoughtful and could well be that of Christopher Wren.

Figure 52

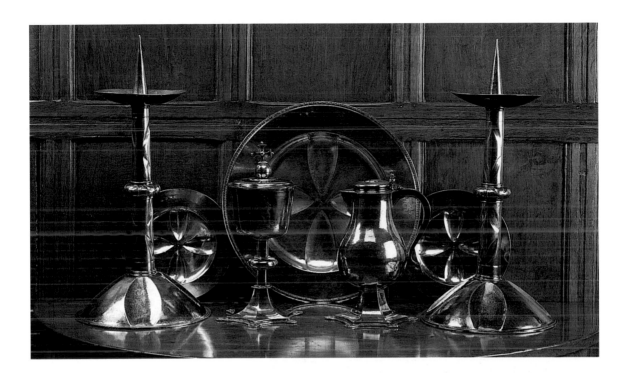

Figure 53 Wren's Chapel plate. Matthew Wren's will provided that Pembroke should have first choice of the furnishings of his chapel at Ely House, Holborn. Items of which Pembroke had no need were to be offered to Jesus College. Among other articles, Pembroke received this chapel plate: an alms dish and a pair of patens, all with a design of four lobes in a well, which matches that of the candlesticks; a chalice and cover, the latter with orb and cross, and a flagon. All silver-gilt and *c.* 1650–60.

Figure 54 Wren's stall cushions. Six of a set of 29 cushions bequeathed by Matthew Wren. They bear the arms of the See of Ely impaling Wren in a cartouche surmounted by a mitre. The cushions were perhaps part of the furnishings of Wren's private chapel at Ely House, Holborn, though since their number agrees very nearly with the number of stalls, they may have been made to Wren's order for the new Chapel. The knotted pile fabric of the cushions is made in the same way as an oriental carpet (so-called 'Turkey work'). They were probably made in Norwich, a known centre for such work in the sixteenth and seventeenth centuries, and are a rare survival.

Figure 55 Altarpiece, *The Entombment*, after Barocci.

THE ALTARPIECE

The painting of *The Entombment* that hangs at the east end of the Chapel is a copy after Barocci. That artist, born in about 1535 in Urbino (where his father, a sculptor, had worked on the great Palazzo Ducale), was the leading central Italian painter of his day.

The original of the altarpiece was painted in 1579–82 for the church of S. Croce in Senigallia, a small town on the Adriatic coast not far from Urbino. The church, as it happens, is not dissimilar to Wren's chapel, and the shape of the original painting, which has a rounded top, closely echoes that of the round-headed windows present in both buildings. The figures are placed in a narrow, ravine-like space bounded by rocks on either side. The body of Christ, lying on a white sheet, is being carried by St John the Evangelist at His feet and by Nicodemus (right) and Joseph of Arimathea at His head. The three men are stepping cautiously forwards with their burden: the body sags, a dead weight. Strongly lit and centrally placed, it is the focus of our attention. Mary Magdalene kneels in the foreground. On the left, placed further back, are the Virgin and two other mourning women. The atmosphere is one of calm and grief after the drama of the Crucifixion. In the original, Calvary rises in the background with Christ's cross placed on the central axis of the painting. To the right in both paintings appears part of the Palazzo Ducale of Urbino. (Today, curiously enough, there is a reduced version of the painting in the Palazzo Ducale itself, now an art gallery.)

The painting rapidly became famous and attracted many copyists. There are significant differences between the College's version and the original. Most obviously, the domed top has gone and with it Calvary. The differences between the pictures as a whole suggest that the copyist had probably never seen the original. On stylistic grounds the copy might be the work of a seventeenth-century north-European artist.

The College's picture has one notable claim to fame: it belonged to Sir Joshua Reynolds. It was bought at Reynolds' sale by Edmund Malone and a year or so later, in about 1797, the painting was given to the College by Dr Richard Baker, who had been briefly a Fellow. We do not know how he acquired it. At the time Baker held a College living as Rector of Cawston, the village in Norfolk where he was born. There is no record of there being an altarpiece in Chapel before Baker's gift: presumably the reredos was bare.

(A shortened version of an article in *PCCS Annual Gazette*, **66** (1992).)

Figure 56 The ends of the book cases in the Old Library (now mostly set against the wall as panelling) all bear richly carved friezes of birds, fruit and flowers.

OLD LIBRARY

After the completion of the new Chapel the medieval Chapel stood disused for twenty-five years until it was decided to convert it into a Library. The conversion was radical, and except for some masonry incorporated into the walls of the new building, nothing remains of its precursor. The Gothic windows were replaced by simple two-light windows on the north and south sides and by a fine Venetian window at the west end. A new ceiling was created by Henry Doogood, plasterer, and paired oak book cases were placed down the length of the room between the windows. The ceiling bears the date 1690, which may be taken as the approximate date for completion of the work. The room was the College's library until 1878, when the Waterhouse Library was completed (see p. 114). The room was then converted into a meeting room (the Old Library, as we now have it). The book cases were mostly dismantled and the ends set against the walls as panelling. (One complete set survives and two half cases set against the east wall.)

The Old Library is still one of the grandest rooms in Cambridge. It achieves this by virtue of the superb ceiling and the high quality of the panelling and the carving on the old book cases. The ceiling is a

Figure 57 Old Library ceiling. At top a putto representing air rides a swan through clouds; below part of a frieze in which putti chase animals through foliage, a centaur to the left.

virtuoso performance by a master craftsman: Doogood was later to work with Wren on the City churches. Like the ceiling of the Chapel, it almost certainly has an allegorical programme, not yet deciphered. There are books in the panels at the two ends. Around the central panel are four putti representing the four elements: earth, air, fire and water. The whole universe, we are perhaps being told, is contained in the books in this room. The central panel itself contains game birds (duck, swan, pheasant, grouse etc.) and the rich borders surrounding it and the other panels are filled with friezes representing the chase: here there are stags, boar, swans, dogs, a centaur and so on. Is it too fanciful to interpret all this as symbolizing the scholar hunting for knowledge?

A. V. Grimstone

Acknowledgements are due to Mr Robert Ferguson for his observations on the Chapel and Old Library decorative schemes.

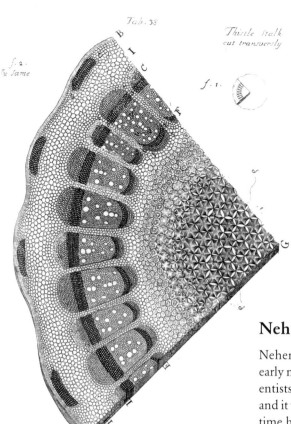

Tab. 38

Thistle Stalk
cut transversely

f. 2.
The Same

f. 1.

Nehemiah Grew

Nehemiah Grew, who graduated from Pembroke in 1661, was an early member of the Royal Society and among the most eminent scientists of his day. He trained in medicine after leaving Cambridge and it was as a physician that he earned his living. However, from the time he was a young man, Grew tells us, he was interested in plants and animals and began to make observations on their structure and functions. While animal anatomy had been closely investigated for many years, the study of plant anatomy had hardly been conceived of; but '. . . both came at first out of the same Hand, and are therefore Contrivances of the same Wisdom', which could be studied as well in the one as in the other. Early in 1671 Grew sent to the Royal Society his first botanical paper. Before the end of the year the Royal Society had undertaken to publish his first book, *The Anatomy of Vegetables Begun*, and had elected him a Fellow. He was later to become curator of its collections and eventually Secretary.

The seventeenth century saw the introduction of the microscope for the study of living organisms. Grew was a pioneer in this field. With his contemporary, Marcello Malpighi, working independently in Italy, he founded the subject of plant anatomy. The minute structure of plants, as it can be seen quite readily with even a modest microscope, was an unexplored world. In the space of ten years Grew produced a stream of publications on the anatomy of roots, stems, leaves, flowers, fruits and seeds, which were gathered together in his masterpiece *The Anatomy of Plants* (1682). His books are illustrated with splendid, remarkably accurate line engravings, full of precisely observed detail. He saw and drew what we now know to be cells, though he had no conception of these as the essential units of which living organisms are constructed. Grew was a scientist, in the modern

Figure 58 Engraving from Grew's greatest work, *The Anatomy of Plants* (London, 1682). The magnificently detailed illustrations of plant structure, such as this drawing of the microscopic structure of the stem of a thistle, could scarcely be bettered today.

sense, observing and experimenting. The slavish dependence on classical authorities is a matter for ridicule, 'as if Aristotle must be brought to prove a Man hath ten Toes'. He was the first to suggest that plants engage in sexual reproduction and that the stamens are the male organs. He also carried out experiments on plant physiology.

Grew worked in other fields, too: appended to his *Catalogue* of the Royal Society's collection there is the text of his lectures on *The Comparative Anatomy of Stomachs and Guts begun*, a landmark in the history of zoology in that it is the first example of the comparative method of study. Grew also investigated the desalination of sea water by distillation, the chemical composition of various natural mineral waters, and fingerprints. His final work was on economics: a statistically based essay on *The Meanes of a most ample Encrease of the Wealth and Strength of England*. In his diversity of interests and his eagerness to observe and experiment, Grew was a typical member of the early Royal Society and a key figure in the seventeenth-century flowering of natural science in England. He died in 1712 while going on his medical rounds. In the words of the sermon preached at his funeral, 'It was his Honour and his Happiness to be Serviceable to the last moments of Life.'

A. V. Grimstone

Richard Crashaw (*c.* 1612–1649)

Crashaw's much-anthologised *Wishes to his Supposed Mistress* is probably his best-known poem, though its lyrical form and lightness of touch are, in fact, more reminiscent of Jonson and Herrick than the more sombre and intense religious poetry that mostly occupied him. He was also a prolific translator into English verse from Latin, Greek and Italian religious and secular poetry; and his secular English poetry was often to mark some formal occasion: panegyric, epithalamium, royal birth, epitaph etc. To his religious work, the term 'baroque' is often applied, and Crashaw's exuberant verses on the physical agonies of Christ and the martyrs and the sorrows of the Virgin owe much to the Continental Catholicism that increasingly attracted him. In *Song upon the Bleeding Crucifix*, Christ's feet 'swim, alas! In their own flood', and the poet laments over Christ's 'deepe dig'd side/That hath a double *Nilus* flowing'. In *A Hymn to St Teresa*, her heart will 'Kisse the sweetly-killing DART!/ And close in his embraces keep/Those delicious Wounds, that weep/Balsom to heal themselves with', etc. This brief article, however, will be confined to some of Crashaw's writing when at Cambridge, and specifically to that which relates to Pembroke.

To understand the pressures on Richard Crashaw's short life, it is first necessary to set this deeply religious man in the context of the time. Richard's father, the Reverend William Crashaw, who died when his son was fourteen, was staunchly Puritan, writing many treatises about the 'fowlest impieties & heresies' of the Roman Catholic Church. The Puritans fiercely mistrusted any observances that smacked of 'Popishness' among the High Churchmen of the Church of England; and Cambridge University was suspected of encouraging Roman Catholic practice. Paranoia reigned. To take an example that was very close to Richard Crashaw's experience, John Cosin, Master of Peterhouse and Vice-Chancellor of the University, instantly disinherited a son who converted to Rome. This speedy action was probably because it was in the new chapel at Peterhouse that pre-Reformation ritual was preserved by Cosin, and he had no desire to offer further ammunition to detractors who regarded such practices as dangerously 'Roman' (though Puritan animosity towards Cosin's High Churchmanship continued for many years).

Crashaw had been elected to a Fellowship at Peterhouse in 1635 and took holy orders in 1638. In the richly decorated chapel of Peterhouse and at Little St Mary's Church, he conducted the services when a catechist and curate. The Laudian ritual of the services brought him also under suspicion, and he had to appear before the Vice-Chancellor's Court on two occasions, one for possessing a copy of Francis de Sales' *L'introduction à la Vie dévote*, which was considered to contain passages that were 'Popish and unsound', the other to answer the charge made by some townspeople that his instruction of catechumens at Little St Mary's was too prolonged. In both cases Crashaw was cleared. In 1643, Crashaw refused to swear the oath of Solemn League and Covenant, and his Fellowship was forcibly terminated the next year. Anticipating the arrival of Cromwell's troops, he fled first to Holland, then France (where he converted to Roman Catholicism) and finally to Italy, where he died in 1649.

Crashaw had entered Charterhouse School when he was sixteen or seventeen. There was, as in all similar schools, a strong emphasis on Classics, and scholars had to write each week four Greek and four Latin epigrams based on the second lesson for the Sunday service. These epigrams (Crashaw had a preference for the four-liners) gave scope for variety of forms and rhetorical devices. He entered Pembroke in 1631, and graduated BA in 1634. When he was twenty-two, he published his *Epigrammatum Sacrorum Liber*, containing 178 Latin epigrams, and these works must have been written at school and at Pembroke. They are polished and often include subtle word-play. The following (based on *St Matthew's Gospel*, chapter 9) is a typical example:

Tu (Pharisæe) nequis in Christo cernere Christum
(You, Pharisee, cannot see the Christ in Christ)

Here Crashaw plays on *Christus* meaning the anointed one, and

Christus meaning Christ himself as person. The death of his friend William Herries, who died in 1631, was lamented by Crashaw in four English poems; and it was Crashaw who wrote the Latin epitaph on Herries, which is to be seen in College in the vestibule of the Old Library. (A complete translation appears on p. 79.) Herries, a graduate of Christ's, died at the age of twenty-three, only a few months after being elected to a fellowship at Pembroke. The epitaph shows that same combination of witty word-play and elegance that appears in the Christus/Christus quoted above. For example, Crashaw remarks on the pleasurable inner rivalry for affection in Herries' mind between his undergraduate College, Christ's, and his Fellowship at Pembroke, and this inter collegiate tension is resolved because Heaven is itself a college, of which 'God made him a fellow', and

Qui et ipse COLLEGIUM fvit
in quo
MUSAE omnes et GRATIAE

(A college he was besides in his own person, uniting all the Muses and Graces.)

Crashaw had been at Pembroke only four months when he wrote this epitaph, and it is some indication of the esteem in which he must have been held that he was commissioned to produce the text for the memorial. The English poem *Upon the Death of Mr. Herrys* depicts Herries as a plant growing high into the clouds with the Muses perching in its branches; now that the tree has died the root alone remains in the earth, buried but immanent with life, ready to rise again. The last lines beg for the sympathetic sorrow of the reader whose tear will enhance the latent life in the dead Herries, now a 'root' in the ground:

Meane while who e're thou art that passest here,
O doe thou water it with one kind Teare.

In general, these elegies are more remarkable for the polish of their form and word-play than for any particular originality of content. There is a play on the idea of Learning (as a personification) in the act of learning:

In him [Herries] Goodness joy'd to see
Learning, learne Humility.

And in the same poem, the passer-by who sees the gravestone will, through being deeply moved by contemplating the virtues of the dead man, transfer him from the grave to entomb him in his heart.

Crashaw's other commemorative poem on a Fellow of Pembroke was written in memory of the great Lancelot Andrewes (see p. 38), Master of Pembroke 1589–1605, who bequeathed to the College

Figure 59 Frontispiece to the 1632 edition of Andrewes' *XCVI Sermons*, Crashaw's poem below. Engraved by John Payne.

See heer a Shadow from that setting SUNNE.
Whose glorious course through this Horizon runn,
Left the dimm face of our dull Hemisphære.
All one great Eye, all drown'd in one great Teare.
Whose rare industrious Soule led his free thought
Through Learning's Universe, and vainly sought
Room for her Spacious Self; until at length
She found ÿ may home with an holy strength

Snatcht herself hence to Heavn: filld a bright place
Midst those immortal Fires, and on the face
Of her Great MAKER fixt a flaming eye.
Where still she reads true, pure Divinitie.
And now ÿ graue Aspect hath deignd to shrink,
Into this lesse appearance. If you think
Tis but a dead face Art doth heer bequeath
Lask on the following leaues & see him breath.

Are to be sold by R. Badger dwelling
in Stationers Hall 1632.

John Payne Fecit

Acknowledgements are due to the following:
George Walton Williams (ed.), *Complete poetry of Richard Crashaw* (1972); Hilton Kelliher, 'Crashaw at Cambridge' in J.R. Roberts (ed.) *New perspectives on the life and art of Richard Crashaw* (1990);
Paul A. Parish, *Richard Crashaw* (1980).

many of the volumes from his magnificent library. An engraving of Andrewes was made for the 1632 reprint of his sermons, with Crashaw's poem engraved below on the same plate (figure 59). It is an elegant poem, and contains the felicitous word-play that is the hallmark of Crashaw's poetry: Andrewes' soul can now for eternity fix her eye on God, 'Where still she [the soul] reads true, pure Divinitie'. The soul of Andrewes now sees God face to face; Andrewes the theologian, student-like, is 'reading divinity' for ever!

Crashaw's mother had died when he was seven, and his step-mother when he was nine. His female friendships tended to be with mother-figures, such as the Countess of Denbigh, Queen Henrietta Maria and Mary Collet (who was in charge of the religious community at Little Gidding, some twenty miles from Cambridge). Many of his poems are dedicated to female saints such as Mary Magdalene and Teresa. Crashaw had good friends, but the passion of his life was religion and religious poetry. There is probably more than just cynical wit in a little epigram *On Marriage*:

I would be married, but I'de have no Wife,
I would be married to a single Life.

Colin Wilcockson

CRASHAW'S EPITAPH FOR WILLIAM HERRIES

The Latin epitaph is inscribed on a monument to William Herries in the vestibule of the Old Library (see above). It was published in Crashaw's *Steps to the Temple*. This translation by Michael Reeve appeared in *PCCS Annual Gazette,* **64** (1990). The date 'MDXXI' in the last line is an unexplained error.

Stay a moment, passer by, where a long stay awaits.
This, be assured, is your destination,
whatever your destination.

It will repay your time
and a tear
to learn that here lies
William Herries,
in whom a distinguished family
attained its greatest distinction.
Acquaint yourself with the life of such a man,
and with its length,
and you will see
to what a height may rise
mortal aspirations
and from what a height fall.
Essex witnessed his childhood,
Cambridge his youth,
neither, alas, his old age.
Alumnus of Christ's College
and fellow of Pembroke Hall,
he stirred up between them a great contest of affection,
until their pleasurable rivalry came to nothing:
of Heaven's College
he had always been an alumnus,
and God made him a fellow.

A college he was besides in his own person,
uniting all the Muses and Graces,
nowhere more truly sisters,
in a bond of close fellowship
under the presidency of Religion.
Oratory acknowledged him as a poet,
poetry as an orator,
both as a philosopher,
and as a Christian all;
he overcame the world by faith,
heaven by hope,
his neighbour by charity,
and himself by humility;
and a youthful brow so cloaked his venerable mind,
easy manners his strict virtue,
manifold talents his meagre years,
and greater modesty his great talents,
that his life
can be called a meek and honourable disguise.
So too his death:
at his burial
he let the narrow confines of this stone
disguise the stature of the sojourner beneath.
The smaller his tomb,
the greater his memorial.

He died on that very day when the lesson at Evensong in the
Church of England says 'he was snatched away lest wickedness
should change his understanding',
namely the 15th of October, in the year of grace 1521.

Figure 60 Brawne's Tankard. 1660/61 and (apart from a recently acquired communion cup) the College's oldest piece of plate after the two medieval cups, all between these dates having been sent to the King in about 1640. Given by Hugh Brawne, admitted Fellow Commoner, 1661.

Figure 61 Bacon's Monteith. A monteith was originally a punch bowl with a separate battlemented rim on which ladle-like cups could be hung and all removed together. This form soon went out of use and the rim was soldered on, as in this example. Date mark 1697/98; maker Anthony Nelme. Given by Sir Edmund Bacon, Fellow Commoner, 1697.

5 THE EIGHTEENTH CENTURY

In this century two of Pembroke's greatest poets – Thomas Gray and Christopher Smart – and its greatest statesman – William Pitt – were in residence. Evidently, the College did not lack distinction, and there were some other notable, though less important, figures. Yet in other respects, and particularly in the second half of the century, this was a sluggish period in the College's history. In Roger Long's reign of thirty-seven years as Master (1733–1770) the total entry was 193; in 1748 only one pensioner was admitted. Gray, writing to his friend Thomas Wharton at that time, says, 'I wish you would send them up some Boys, for they are grown extremely thin from their late long Indisposition' The unhurried pace of Pembroke life at this time is confirmed by the near absence of building activity.

Buildings

From 1712 the walls of Old Court, a crumbling mixture of rubble and plaster, were faced with Ketton stone. Chapel Court was unsightly on its east side, where the Master's Lodge, as shown in Loggan's view (p. 54), presented a blank wall to the Court, with a covered staircase providing the Master with access to the Chapel. In 1745, during Roger Long's mastership, a new entrance front was built in the court (figure 64). Subdued Georgian in style, and built of brick, it was the design of Greaves, a local mason. Inside was a hall and staircase. It was only two storeys high: behind it towered the older lodging, with its impressive three-storey bay window facing south over the Master's garden. The Master's drawing room lay behind the first-floor bay window; below it was the kitchen, and other domestic offices occupied the rest of the ground floor, including part of the south range of Old Court. The photograph of the Lodge from the garden (figure 62) shows its rambling character, for behind the tall lodging was the south end of the Hall, with the Fellows' parlour on the ground floor, the audit room or Master's dining room on the first floor, and two floors of rooms above. These were reached from the turret stair, just visible in the picture.

Figure 62 The Master's Lodge and adjoining buildings from the garden. At left the east end of the Chapel as built by Wren (i.e. before Scott's extension). The ivy-clad rectangular building next to it is the side of the eighteenth-century extension of the Lodge (see figure 64), while next to that is the three-storey bay window of the older Lodge. To the right of the tree is the end of the medieval Hall; above the left-hand side of the gable can be seen the top of the turret stair referred to in the text. Finally, at the right the west end of Hitcham Building (i.e. the south range of Ivy Court) can be seen.

Figure 63 Plan showing the arrangement of buildings as they existed up to 1870. (From Willis and Clark, *Architectural History of the University of Cambridge*.)

Figure 64 The eighteenth-century west front of
the Master's Lodge, with the steep roof and tall
bay window of the older part of the Lodge
behind. On the left is part of the south range of
Old Court (all demolished 1874).

Roger Long 1680–1770

'At this time, and for many years to come, the Master of Pembroke was a richly eccentric figure named Roger Long. He was a Norfolk man by birth, a Tory in a society predominantly Whig, obstinate and cantankerous in temper, an astronomer and a musician with a lifelong addiction to scientific experiments of every kind.' (R.W. Ketton-Cremer, *Thomas Gray.*)

Long was one of the 'characters' of eighteenth-century Cambridge. He was Master of Pembroke, Vice-Chancellor, Fellow of the Royal Society and first Lowndean Professor of Astronomy and Geometry. His long and not untroubled reign as Master was notable for a prolonged quarrel with the Fellows in 1746–49. An ingenious inventor, Long constructed in his garden a large pond, which a contemporary observer commended as 'a beautiful and large Bason', wherein 'he often diverts himself in a Machine of his own contrivance, to go with the Foot as he rides therein'. Unfortunately, no illustration of this water-bicycle or its intrepid rider seems to have been preserved. The imperfect construction

Figure 65 Roger Long: portrait by Benjamin Wilson, painted in Long's 89th year.

Roger Long's Great Sphere

An early version of a planetarium, perhaps at the time the largest ever constructed. It was a hollow sphere, 18 feet in diameter and made of copper. Turned by a winch, it represented on its inner surface the apparent movements of the heavenly bodies. Thirty people could sit in it. The Sphere was originally housed in a building on the site of Pitt Buildings (M staircase). It was moved into the garden when the Old Master's Lodge (now N staircase) was built and the site was wanted for stables. The Sphere survived for over a century before being broken up. In this photograph, taken in 1871, John Power, Master, stands at the left.

Figure 66

of the pond was blamed when the chapel vault was opened in 1770 to deposit Long's coffin, and was found to be flooded.

In some ways scarcely less remarkable than Long was his assistant, Richard Dunthorne, who deserves the place he has won in the *Dictionary of National Biography.* Dunthorne was the discovery of Roger Long, who took him from Ramsey in Huntingdon to be his footboy. He improved his education and became schoolmaster at Coggeshall in Essex, after which he returned to the service of the College, and was appointed butler in 1743. However, his activities ranged far beyond the Buttery. He was the Master's scientific assistant, helped in the construction of the Great Sphere, and managed the printing-press on which Long was printing his astronomical works. Himself an astronomer of no mean ability, he published many of his observations including his *Practical Astronomy of the Moon* (Cambridge, 1739). He was left by Long the task of completing his astronomical work. He resigned the post of butler in 1771, at which time he had become superintendent of the works of the Bedford Level.

(Adapted from a passage in an article by Leonard Whibley, 'The Jubilee at Pembroke Hall in 1743', *Blackwood's Magazine*, 1927, reprinted in *PCCS Annual Gazette*, **48** (1974)).

Sir Benjamin Keene

'The most eminent of the British ministers sent to Spain in the eighteenth century', Benjamin Keene was born in King's Lynn and came up to Pembroke in 1713. Through the influence of Sir Robert Walpole he was appointed agent for the South Sea Company at Madrid. In 1724 he became British consul there and in 1727 minister plenipotentiary. Horace Walpole described him as, 'one of the best kind of agreeable men, quite fat and easy, with universal knowledge.'

Figure 67 Sir Benjamin Keene (1697–1757). Artist unknown.

Smart and Gray

Christopher Smart had an odd sense of timing. In January 1756, seven years after he left Cambridge for London, he published a celebratory *Secular Ode on the Jubilee at Pembroke College, Cambridge, in 1743* (printed in full below), addressed to its Foundress, which ends:

> Let others, with enthusiasm fill'd,
>   Nunneries and convents build;
> Where, decay'd with fasts and years,
>   Melancholy loves to dwell,
>   Moaping in her midnight cell,
> And counts her beads, and mumbles o'er th'unmeaning prayers.
>   Religious joy, and sober pleasure,
>   Virtuous ease, and learned leisure,
>   Society and books, that give
>   Th'important lesson how to live:
>   These are gifts, are gifts divine,
>   For, fair Pembroke, these were thine.

But Smart spoke too soon against religious 'enthusiasm' (a word that then suggested stepping dangerously beyond the bounds of reason). A month after this poem's publication he was struck down by illness, and when he recovered his own 'Religious joy' had become manically enthusiastic. Taking seriously the Biblical suggestion that he 'pray without ceasing', Smart began praying whenever and wherever the mood took him, falling on his knees in the street or knocking on his friends' doors in the middle of the night. Wholly unembarrassed by nudges and stares, he rejoiced in God not in 'mumbles' but in a powerful bass voice: 'I am the Reviver of ADO-RATION amongst ENGLISH-MEN'. His friends found him less than adorable, as a disturbing gap was opened between their understanding of prayer as something privately recited to aid forgiving, and his own prayers which were meant simply for giving, whether asked for or not. By May 1757, he had been admitted to St Luke's Hospital for the Insane, where he wrote the crazed fragments of *Jubilate Agno*, a dazzling catalogue of the glories of creation, which included memories of his old College's foundation on a bedrock of faith:

For all Foundation is from God depending.
For the two Universities are the Eyes of England.
For Cambridge is the right and the brightest.
For Pembroke Hall was founded more in the Lord than any other
     College in Cambridge.

Later in his life he had good reason to be thankful not only for 'gifts divine' but also for the smaller mercies of money, many Fellows of Pembroke loyally adding their names to his subscription lists in an unsuccessful attempt to save him from the debtor's prison.

Among his supporters was another poet, Thomas Gray (who had moved from Peterhouse to Pembroke in 1756), which seems strange when gossip has it that they loathed one another. Perhaps it was poetic jealousy, or a case of too many (two) bright young things in a small College, or even the fact that they couldn't avoid seeing eye to eye when they were both so short. Certainly, the prim and fussy Gray despaired of Smart's 'Lies, Impertinence and Ingratitude' (the last a measured swipe at the man who had written poems with titles like *Munificence and Modesty* and *On Gratitude*), and took a grim pleasure in prophesying as early as 1747 that Smart 'must come to a Jayl, or Bedlam, and that without any help, almost without pity'. Almost, but not quite, because the two poets also had much – perhaps, for Gray, too much – in common, going beyond their shared fondness for cats, or Aeolian lyres, or the poetry of Alexander Pope (both met him; the College's portrait of Smart has him proudly showing off Pope's letter). There are also points of contact in their lives at Pembroke which are sunk deep in the imaginative preoccupations of their writing.

Figure 68 Thomas Gray. Silhouette by Francis Mapletoft, Fellow.

One is a strained sense of, and sensitivity to, confinement. When Gray notes in a letter that Smart cannot live 'within bounds', and has been 'confin'd to his rooms' so as to avoid a swarm of creditors, it is with a curious mix of envy and apprehensiveness, having spent much of his own life snugly cocooned in the same College rooms, and much of this time in despair at his limited horizons. 'I'm like a cabbage', he once wrote, 'where I'm stuck, I love to grow', as if being confined was something he was stuck with rather than something he chose to stick out, pottering around his rooms and growing mosses or tending to his pet owl. Always 'the same dull prospect', he sighs, meaning always the same old view out of his window, and no danger of removing himself from it; 'having made four-and-twenty steps more', he adds, 'I shall be just where I was', as though the 'little, waddling Fresh-man of Peterhouse' was turning into not a cabbage but an elderly hamster puffing away on the wheel of the academic year. Gray was only nineteen when he wrote this, but in a sense he was already much older. Other men might dread turning into their fathers. Gray was only waiting to grow into himself, looking forward to the time when he would have enough material to look back and brood for real over his lifelong sense of loss. His poems too reflect his mixed feelings about withdrawing from the messy world outside into the neat but deadening routines of College life. *Ode on a Distant Prospect of Eton College* describes a 'captive linnet' in order to suggest the 'constraint' put on schoolboys doomed to grow up, and 'The limits of their little reign'; the 'secret bow'r' of the owl in *Elegy Written in a Country Church-Yard* turns the 'narrow cell' of the closed graves into a cosy refuge as well as a chilly prison. In each case, Gray's anguished pleasure in thoughts of being shut in or shut up

Figure 69 The opening lines of Gray's *Elegy Written in a Country Church-yard* in a manuscript copy in his commonplace books (vol. 2. p.617). This is one of three autograph manuscripts of the poem. Gray's commonplace books, in three large volumes, were bequeathed to Pembroke by Richard Stonhewer of Peterhouse, a friend of Gray, together with portraits of Gray and William Mason. The commonplace books contain a miscellany of Gray's notes on his reading, extracts from classical and other authors, autograph versions of many of his own poems, and much else.

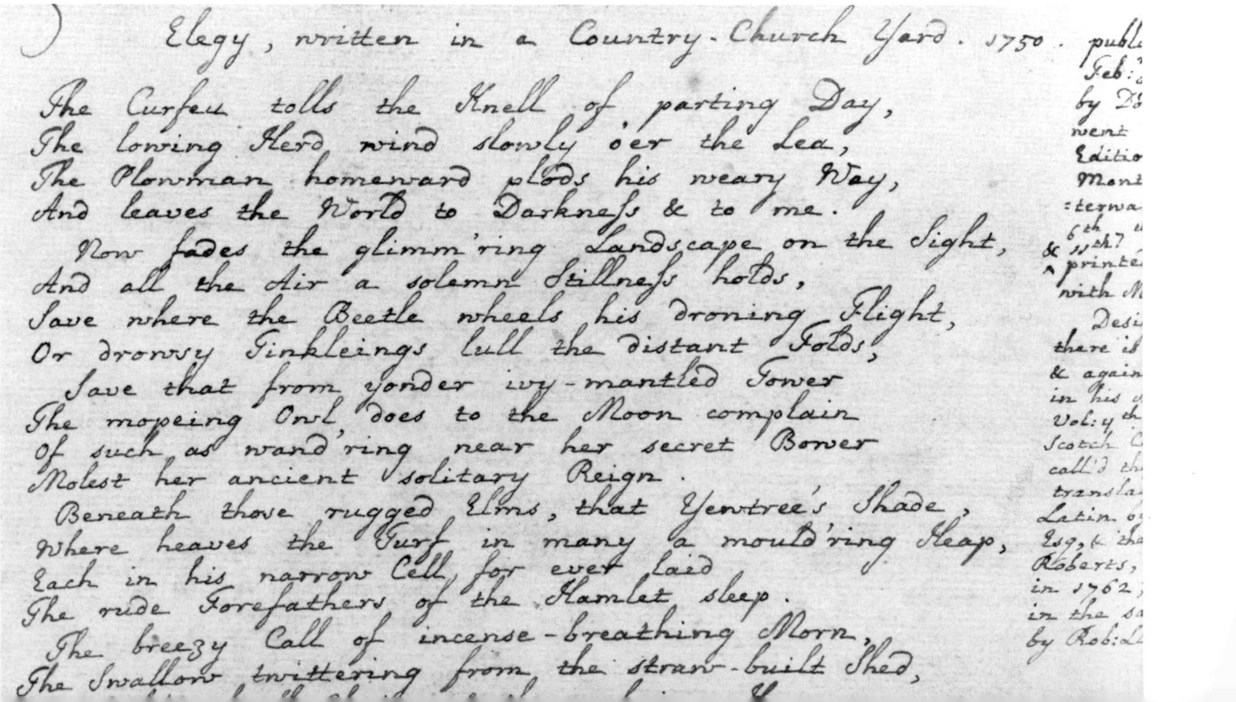
Elegy, written in a Country-Church Yard. 1750.

The Curfeu tolls the Knell of parting Day,
The lowing Herd wind slowly o'er the Lea,
The Plowman homeward plods his weary Way,
And leaves the World to Darkness & to me.
Now fades the glimm'ring Landscape on the Sight,
And all the Air a solemn Stillness holds,
Save where the Beetle wheels his droning Flight,
Or drowsy Tinkleings lull the distant Folds;
Save that from yonder ivy-mantled Tower
The mopeing Owl does to the Moon complain
Of such as wand'ring near her secret Bower
Molest her ancient solitary Reign.
Beneath those rugged Elms, that Yewtree's Shade,
Where heaves the Turf in many a mould'ring Heap,
Each in his narrow Cell for ever laid
The rude Forefathers of the Hamlet sleep.
The breezy Call of incense-breathing Morn,
The Swallow twittering from the straw-built Shed,

Dr William Oliver

Dr Oliver, physician, was a Cornishman and came up to Pembroke in 1714. He completed his training at Leyden and settled in Bath, where he took a prominent part in the medical life of the city. He is remembered as the inventor of the Bath Oliver biscuit, still made today and which bears his silhouette. His coachman Atkins, to whom he confided the recipe, opened a shop to sell the biscuits and acquired a large fortune.

Figure 70

would have chimed with Smart, who before his own incarceration wrote *On an Eagle Confined in a College Court*, and in his early prize poems turned with relief from seeing God in an 'unbounded prospect' to seeing Him in echoing 'enclosures' like towers and caves. Rumour had it that Gray's eleven brothers and sisters had all died young of suffocation, which might account for his terror of being trapped in his rooms by fire and its choking smoke, something Smart should have been especially sympathetic to after having written a peculiar epilogue to *Othello* in which the smothered Desdemona gets up to explain, 'I come to speak in spight of Suffocation . . . We may be choak'd, but never can be dumb'. Perhaps Gray's fear of suffocation also suggests why he found completing poems painful or impossible. The Italian word 'stanza' literally means 'a room', an enclosed place in which words can settle into comfortable routines of speech and breathing, and although Smart occasionally borrowed Gray's 'Elegy' stanza form, as one might hire a room for a party, Gray himself increasingly preserved his poems unfinished, as if leaving for himself an escape route on paper like the rope-ladder he famously installed on his window-ledge at Peterhouse. A note for one poem reads: 'All that men of power can do for men of genius is to leave them at their liberty, compared to birds that, when confined to a cage, do but regret the loss of their freedom in melancholy strains'. The poem was never written, perhaps because Gray realised that he was already living it in Cambridge; as he wrote in the *Elegy*, 'Melancholy mark'd him for her own'.

Unlike Smart's 'Melancholy', however, Gray didn't simply mope in his cell. 'Travel I must, or cease to exist', he later explained, but away from his stately walks around Pembroke's gardens, most of his travelling was done indoors, by the regular exercise of his hand, writ-

William Mason (opposite)

Mason was a Fellow of the College, friend and biographer of Gray. He was later prebendary of York Minster. He was a poet (his monument in Westminster Abbey stands next to Gray's), amateur of the arts, garden designer, minor architect and musician – a figure of some importance in the eighteenth century. *The English Garden* (1772–1777), his major poetical work, is a didactic poem inspired by Virgil's *Georgics* and contains his theories of gardening. He designed, or helped to design, the gardens of half a dozen major country houses. Mason was Gray's literary executor and editor of his poems (1775). The memoir of Gray prefixed to the poems pioneered the idea of biography through 'life and letters'. Mason's portrait, by Sir Joshua Reynolds, is the best in the College's collection.

Figure 71 William Mason: by Sir Joshua Reynolds (1774; detail).

ing. His compulsion to select and order fragments of the world on paper is a second preoccupation he shared with Smart, who once admitted 'I cannot afford to be idle'. In the asylum, Smart's doctor (the unfortunately named Battie) encouraged routine activities that kept the brain quietly ticking over, like counting lines on paper or copying out names. Smart's prize-winning Cambridge poem *On the Immensity of the Supreme Being* had earlier asked readers to 'List ye! how nature with ten thousand tongues / Begins the grand thanksgiving', and although 'list' here means 'listen', in *Jubilate Agno* it becomes something more like 'list them', as each day in his cell he picked out a single creature or object (ants, say, or mustard, or clarinets) and added a single verse of praise to his list of blessings to be counted. As the list swells, Smart seems in part a prisoner, chalking up the last days of his captivity on the cell wall, and in part a lover, enjoying what E. M. Forster was to call love's sudden exaltation of relevance. We might suspect similar motives behind Gray's need to copy down chunks of his reading and fill in forms with data, busily preventing himself from becoming one of those 'sleepy, drunken, dull, illiterate Things' who surrounded him, like a wall of black gowns. His large commonplace books, still held by Pembroke, often read like a secular *Jubilate Agno*, diaries crammed with small notes on everything from Danish food to what one should do if bitten by a viper, from calendars of the weather to what he once discovered in the body of a dead mole. One letter has a lovingly detailed recipe for the famous pot pourri that scented his rooms, and reading his long lists of local flora and fauna we can see why. To a mind that brooded on the 'Ample page / Rich with the spoils of time', as well as what time spoils, his brimming jar of pot pourri could preserve the rich natural world in miniature, like a commonplace book full of pressed flowers.

It's a touching idea, that pot pourri can keep you sane, but also the kind of thing that could easily get up the nose of someone closer to madness. A witticism about Gray's mincing steps and disdainful air was attributed to Smart: 'Gray *walks* as if he had fouled his small-clothes, and *looks* as if he smelt it'. If this is Smart's, the schoolboy tittering about 'smalls' does at least hint at that eye for the little and the hidden, which both poets enjoyed. 'The Lord magnify the idea of Smart singing hymns on this day in the eyes of the whole University of Cambridge Novr. 5th 1762' is one sad daydream in *Jubilate Agno*, which is forever magnifying the world as if seeing it through a microscope as well as hearing of it through prayer. But Gray too saw the little and large in one another: sending his first impressions of Cambridge to Walpole, he grumbles Eyeorishly about 'a great old Town, shaped like a Spider, with a nasty lump in the middle of it, & half a dozen scrambling long legs'. Out of Cambridge he is still bored, 'It rains, 'tis Sunday, this is the country'. Smart wrote

Figure 72 (opposite) Christopher Smart (1722–71). Smart plainly intended this portrait to give an impression as far removed as possible from that conveyed by Gray in his letters. Handsomely dressed, he is shown seated, pen in hand, against a background of learned works. On the table by his side is a letter with the signature, 'Alexander Pope'. The envelope addressed to 'Mr Smart, Pemb. Hall, Cambridge' is also prominently displayed. The painting came to the College in 1925, the gift of Miss Cowslade, 'his last descendant'. Artist unknown.

comedies for a living, but jokes aren't quite what we expect from the melancholic Gray. In fact, history has largely gone along with the hints dropped by their names: Smart was smart, Gray was just dull grey. Still, Gray's friend Walpole once said that 'humour was his natural and original turn', and he certainly needed a sense of humour in Pembroke. Gray had stomped across to Pembroke celebrated as the man who couldn't take a practical joke (some undergraduates had shouted 'Fire!' in the hope of seeing this dignified man shin down the rope-ladder in his nightshirt), but in his correspondence he glumly enjoyed making himself a figure of fun, the sad clown who prophesied that he would be found dead with his head in a chamber-pot. Even his great *Elegy* takes itself seriously enough to wonder whether it might not be taken altogether seriously, the line 'The rude Forefathers of the hamlet sleep' mischievously conjuring up the ghost of Shakespeare's funniest tragedy, *Hamlet*, with its rude gravediggers and restless forefathers. And it is when we read Smart on Gray's airs, or Gray's poker faced asides on Smart's fondness for the bottle, that for a moment we can see them both as they might have been: not as two solemn poets, but as an eighteenth-century double-act, 'Smart and Gray', the funny man and his stooge working their audience together as Pembroke's own Odd Couple.

Robert Douglas-Fairhurst

Gray's commonplace books

He yearn'd to share our young men's hopefulness,
　　And from their gracious mothers learn'd to pray[1];
　　The College did her utmost to redress
　　The load that on her great adopted lay.
　　She gave him Wharton, constant as the day;
　　Mason, musician, artist, gardener,
　　And poet in the friendly eyes of Gray;
　　His little Roman, Brown[2]; and Stonehewer,

　　Who left this wondrous heirloom in the hands
　　Of us, the Masters. Well he might forget
　　From time to time, amidst their genial strife
　　Of wit and worth, the inexorable bands
　　That nature tied for him unborn. And yet
Heigh ho! it was a solitary life.[3]

from A. J. Mason *Pembroke Sonnets*

1 'I would wish to be like Mr Bonfoy, and think that everything turns out the best in the world, but it won't do, I am stupid and low-spirited': (Gray's *Letters*). Ambrose Bonfoy, of Abbot's Ripton, was a Fellow Commoner of Pembroke. His mother was the 'Mrs Bonfoy (who taught me to pray)'.
2 Mr Brown 'wants nothing but a foot in height and his own hair, to make him a little old Roman' (Gray's *Letters*).
3 'Heigh ho! I feel . . . that I have very little to say': (Gray's *Letters*).

CHRISTOPHER SMART *Secular Ode on the Jubilee at Pembroke College Cambridge in 1743*

I

God of science, light divine,
O'er all the world of learning shine;
 Shine fav'ring from th'etherial way:
But here with tenfold influence dwell,
Here all thy various rays compell
 To dignify this joyful day.
Nor thou, *Melpomene*, thy aid refuse,
Nor leave behind the comic muse;
 Mirthful mild, and gravely gay,
 Hither from your thrones away.
And thou, jolly *Bacchus*, shalt haste to come down,
While the full-flowing cup with fresh flow'rets we crown;
 But boast not here thy madding influence,
  For close beside thee *Pallas*' self shall stand,
  And hold thy temerarious hand,
 Forbidding rage to triumph over sense.
 And ye, illustrious-sacred shades,
 Who whilom in these muse-resounding glades,
  High in rapture wont to stray,
  Or trim the learned lamp, till dawn of day,
  Ye blessed sons of happier fates,
  Deign to look down from heav'n and see
  How lasting sweet the memory,
 Which to eternal fame fair virtue consecrates.
See, still fresh bloom your names thro' every age,
Still greatly live along the speaking page.

II

But chiefly thou, *Dan Spencer*, peerless bard,
 Sith in these pleasaunt groves you 'gan devise,
Of Red-cross knight, and virtue's high reward,
 And here first plann'd thy works of vast emprize,
Descend! nor thy inferior sons despise,
 Chaunting her praises on this festal day,
Who taught us, where the road to honour lies,
 Her steps still marking out the arduous way:
Blest is the theme I ween, and blessed be the lay.

III

Behold, in virtue, and in beauty's pride,
Behold, at once, a widow and a bride!
See all the nuptial revels at a stand,

And *Hymen's* torch in *Libitina's* hand,
O what a scene!...
    But, yonder, from on high, descend
  Religion, orphan-virtue's firmest friend,
      And laurell'd learning, mistress of the muse,
  Who, o'er the arts, sits on an eminence,
  By genius erected, and by sense,
      And with unbounded prospect all things views.
  With gentle hands they raise her drooping head,
And bid her trust in heav'n, nor wail the happy dead.
  All that is great and good she now pursues;
  She meditates a mansion for the muse,
    Nor will she lose a day;
  To you religion, wisdom and to you,
  She gives that prime, which pleasure calls her due,
    And folly wastes in wantonness away.
  She, by no specious flow'rs beguil'd,
  That deck *imagination's wild,*
    And witless youth decoy,
  Chose learning's *cultivated* glades,
  And virtue's *ever-blooming* shades,
    That give alone true joy.

IV

  To *Granta* now, where gentle *Camus* laves,
  The reedy shore, and rolls his silver waves,
    She flies, and executes, with bounteous hand,
    The work her mighty soul had plann'd,
  And unborn minds she forms, and future souls she saves,
And to ensure that work to endless fame,
Left what can never die, her own illustrious name.
      Let others, with enthusiasm fill'd,
      Nunneries and convents build;
Where, decay'd with fasts and years,
      Melancholy loves to dwell,
      Moaping in her midnight cell,
And counts her beads, and mumbles o'er th'unmeaning pray'rs.
  Religious joy, and sober pleasure,
  Virtuous ease, and learned leisure,
  Society and books, that give
  Th'important lesson how to live:
  These are gifts, are gifts divine,
  For, fair Pembroke, these were thine.

Figure 73 Godolphin Cup. Given by William
Godolphin, Fellow Commoner.
A dolphin forms part of the crest of
Godolphin. Maker David Willaume (1715–16).

Figure 74 Three of a set of ten mugs. The
inscriptions contain the names of seventeenth-
century donors of earlier pieces, for which the
mugs were obtained in exchange. Maker Alice
Sheen (1710).

Figure 75 Lord Strathmore's candelabrum.
Given by John Lyon, Earl of Strathmore,
Fellow Commoner, 1755. Maker Lewis Black
(1762).

Loggan's engraving of 1682 (p. 54) shows the Bowling Green; it is not known when it was first laid down. In the past Fellows often had their own bowls, several of which survive. These are dated 1760. 'JB' denotes James Brown, who succeeded Roger Long as Master; 'FM' was Francis Mapletoft, who made the silhouette of Gray (p. 87). The Bowling Green is still used today and was returfed in 1996.

Figure 76

William Pitt

William Pitt, the youngest and second longest-serving of British prime ministers, was admitted to Pembroke in April 1773, and resided at intervals over the next seven years. His father, now Earl of Chatham, had chosen the college because the family tutor, Edward Wilson, was a Pembroke man, whose brother was a Fellow. The young Pitt arrived in October 1773, at the tender age of fourteen. He had been educated at home, because his father had 'scarcely observed a boy who was not cowed for life' by being sent away to school. Brought up in a strongly political household, inheriting his father's self-confidence, and possessed of unusual powers of learning, Pitt was not out of place in a college environment. Wilson foretold that he 'will go to Pembroke, not a weak boy to be made a property of, but to be admir'd as a prodigy; not to hear lectures, but to spread light'. His grounding in classics, history and mathematics was already secure, and his memory was exceptional; he 'seemed never to learn, but merely to recollect'.

Pitt was given a set over the Senior Parlour, the rooms of Wilson's brother and before him of Thomas Gray, after whom they are now named. Wilson resided with him until 1775 when he left the family to become a rector in Berkshire. In his first autumn, Pitt quickly fell seriously ill, and had to be attended by the family nurse and by Chatham's doctor Addington. The nurse is said to have lived for some time in the rooms above Pitt's, while it was at this juncture, probably, that Addington prescribed 'liberal potations of port-wine' to the young convalescent. He adhered to this advice throughout his life, which was almost certainly shortened by it; he died at the age of 46.

Pitt was delicate as a youth, and it seems to have been decided that

Figure 77 William Pitt. Detail from the painting by G. H. Harlow, 1812, after the portrait by Hoppner painted in 1805, the year before Pitt's death.

the Cambridge climate was too severe for him except in summer, so in 1774 and 1775 he resided principally during the long vacation. This, together with his age and rank (only eight of the 55 undergraduates admitted to Pembroke between 1773 and 1779 had Pitt's status of fellow-commoner), ensured that he mixed with dons rather than other students. His college tutor was Samuel May, a gossipy Cornishman of little profundity, and from 1775, with Wilson no longer on the premises, Pitt studied most with a young Fellow George Pretyman (later Tomline). Tomline remained Pitt's devoted adherent through life, acquiring in consequence the Bishopric of Lincoln and the Deanery of St Paul's, as well as the right to produce an unreadable official biography. As the son of a peer, Pitt was allowed to become Master of Arts without taking the BA examination, and did this in 1776; he had not kept enough terms to qualify for the BA.

From 1776 until 1779 he continued to reside for several months each year, and now lived much more the life of a normal, albeit

Figure 78 The Pitt Tureen. Given by William Pitt, 1784. The stork and anchor form the Pitt crest. Makers Wakelin & Taylor (1778).

studious, undergraduate of rank. His closest friends were usually of noble birth; only a few, such as E. J. Eliot (who married his sister), were at Pembroke. They were not overmuch given to athletic or bibulous pursuits; they tended to share Pitt's already marked commitment to public affairs. Pitt's intellectual interests reflected this conscious training for political life. His thirst for the classics educated him in oratorical style; his love of the detail of translation and the rigour of mathematics and natural philosophy prepared him for a career of administrative and financial reform. Contemporary literature and French philosophy had nothing of the same fascination for him; his was a practical, not an unusually imaginative mind. A political career was always his for the taking, and after his father's death in 1778 his attention turned increasingly to the London world, though Cambridge continued to claim much of his time until he took chambers in Lincoln's Inn in 1780. In the same year, he was an unsuccessful parliamentary candidate for Cambridge University; in 1781 he became MP for a pocket borough; at the election of 1784 he was returned for the University, Pembroke voting solidly for him. The year before, he had resided briefly and for the last time. Now, in gratitude for his time there, he gave the college a silver soup tureen, surmounted with the family crest. It marked his graduation into the world of affairs – an astonishingly swift one, for he was already Prime Minister, and was to remain so for over seventeen years.

Jonathan Parry

Letter in the College library from Chatham to Joseph Turner, Tutor, dated 9 October 1773, which preceded Pitt's entry into Pembroke.

Sir,

Apprehensions of gout, about this season, forbid my undertaking a journey to Cambridge with my Son. I regret this more particularly, as it deprives me of an occasion of being introduced to your Personal Acquaintance, and that of the Gentlemen of your Society, a loss I shall much wish to repair, at some other time. Mr Wilson, whose admirable Instruction, and affectionate Care have brought my Son, early to receive such further advantages, as he cannot fail to find under your eye, will present Him to you. He is of a tender Age, and of a health not yet firm enough to be indulged, to the full, in the strong desire he has to acquire useful knowledge. An ingenious mind and docility of temper will, I know, render him conformable to your Discipline, in all points. Too young for the irregularities of a man, I trust, he will not, on the other hand, prove troublesome by the Puerile sallies of a Boy. Such as he is I am happy to place him at Pembroke, and I need not say, how much of his Parents Hearts goes along with him.

I am with great esteem and regard,

Sir

your most faithful and most obedient humble Servant,

CHATHAM.

Pitt's rooms

The man was England. Not since Cromwell's time
   Had England spoken with a voice like Pitt's,
   Nor ever any served her more sublime
   In disregard of selfish benefits.
   These isles all one, America at quits,
   Europe deliver'd, – such reward he sought;
   But that dishonest field of Austerlitz
Kill'd him and brought his work, it seem'd, to nought.

   Less tragic, here, we love the pale, frail boy
   In his blue frock, so young, so studious, plied
   With Douro wine against the ancestral curse
   That rack'd him, and yet ready to enjoy
   A puerile sally, lodged where Gray had died,
And with him lodged his tutor and his nurse.

from A. J. Mason: *Pembroke Sonnets*

College life in the eighteenth century

The two letters printed below were edited by W. A. Camps and published in the *PCCS Annual Gazette*, **II** (1937). They were written by Henry Ainslie (1760–1834), who came up to Pembroke in 1777. His father, Dr James Ainslie, a medical practitioner of Kendal, sent three sons to Cambridge. The eldest, Montagu Farrer, went to Trinity and was bracketed second Wrangler in 1781, the same year in which Henry was Senior Wrangler. The third son, Gilbert, came up to Pembroke later and was last of the Wranglers in 1786. All became Fellows of their respective Colleges. Henry took to medicine and became physician to St Thomas's Hospital. He was the father of Gilbert Ainslie, another Pembroke man, who was eighth Wrangler in 1815 and Master of Pembroke from 1828 to 1870 (see p. 110). The first letter was written soon after Henry came into residence and describes his early experiences and impressions. The spelling and punctuation of the originals has been retained.

I FROM HENRY AINSLIE TO HIS FATHER

Hon[d] Father,

I receiv'd your letter with one from my Mother enclos'd yesterday & take this first opportunity of answering them. I have been particularly careful in buying nothing superflous in the furniture of my rooms, as I don't expect to continue in them above half a year, & probably shall find many things useful tho not at present absolutely necessary in the rooms I shall remove to; I have got nothing yet but what I want constantly. I find we are oblig'd at this College to pay for our china & glasses of every kind out of our own pocket, which is not the custom at Trinity & most of the other Colleges, they cost me without buying any thing but what I always want above a Guinea. You desire me to write you an account of my examinations, I have had so many, that to enlarge upon them wou'd fill my letter so I'll give you the heads. Mr. Turner[1] the Mathematical Lecturer first examin'd me in Cicero's Orations Homer & Sophocles, in all which he said he was perfectly satisfied & paid me some compliments; having told him I had been reading Euclid he examin'd me in the 1st & 2nd books & about a week after in the 3[d], in a few days after in the 4th & part of the 5th, & I expect next week or perhaps before, he will examine me in the remainder of the 5th & the 6th. Hitherto he has been so perfectly satisfied with my performance, that he says I need not go to lectures in Euclid at all, but gain a whole year & attend the 2[d] years lectures with the Gentleman of the year above, I hope this will be of some consequence, I have inform'd Dr Watson[2], who seem'd rather

Figure 79 Henry Ainslie (1760–1834) by Thomas
Stewardson.

afraid of his putting me too forward but as he has not examin'd me he can't be so proper a judge as the Tutor. I was also examin'd by the Classical Lecturer[3] who is an exceeding clever man, in the Preface to Catilines conspiracy in Sallust, & Demosthenes, he was just as polite as the other. We shall attend him in Longinus & Quintilian in about a week when all the freshmen are up. The Master[4] of the College who is very intimate with Dr. Watson sends for the freshmen to breakfast one by one, & after breakfast examines them, I was sent for in my turn & examin'd in Tully's Offices & Xenopohons Mirabilia. The story in them both is the same, & he chooses it as an oblique method of telling us, that we can obtain nothing without pains & labour, he is an exceeding good natur'd man. There are at this College about 24 Undergraduates & about 14 Fellows & Fellow Commoners, we have a younger son of Lord Chatham's, who is reckon'd pretty clever[5]. What we call our Commons extends only to the meat kind, if we want roots of any kind, we send for them to the cook, this is what we call sizing, we have three guineas allow'd a quarter for sizing out of which we pay for our suppers, they have only a Guinea & half at Trinity but they don't pay for suppers, they are included in commons, so we are pretty near equal, but it is very rare that the money allow'd us serves, I believe mine will for I don't often eat suppers, at Trinity it never does it is impossible, & what is very extraordinary Monty's bill which the cook brings to him to pay out of his own pocket, after they are out of sizings, that is after they have already had to the value of a Guinea & half, only came to £1.17s. in three quarters, & there is scarce a person whose bill does not exceed that every quarter, it wou'd even been impossible for him to have liv'd so cheap, if he had not as he himself confesses, been such a puppy for 8 months as hardly ever to shew his head. There is not a Pensioner in Trinity but himself who does not get 6 guineas a quarter at least, he seems astonish'd himself how he has done but it is easily accounted for, if he never scarce saw company. It is very odd he is acquainted with all the clever Undergraduates in Cambridge almost, to all of whom he has introduced me, so instead of living retir'd as he did I am in spite of myself engaged with a great number of acquaintances, however we rarely visit, & avoid company as much as possible. This College is very sober & regular as much so as any in Cambridge if not more, which is of great consequence, & has gain'd it a great Character. I can recollect nothing more to tell you only that you may depend upon our living as cheap & regular as we possibly can & I hope & am pretty certain you will never have occasion to complain. The remainder of my letter I must dedicate to my Mother the shortness of which as necessity oblig'd me to mention what I have already wrote, I hope she will excuse. I have receiv'd my parcel by Mr Green with whom we supp'd but had not much conversation because of more company who were constantly with him. My surplice I receiv'd a fortnight ago, it suits very well tho not made quite in Cambridge stile. The principal thing I have to mention is that the gentleman here almost to a man wear ruffled shirts, Monty was oblig'd to get his ruffled, except a few that were ruffled before he came which was rather expensive, if therefore you have not sent my shirts off before you get this I can wait a week very easily longer if you can ruffle them in that time I shall pay much dearer for them here than you can get them done for at Kendal so I think it of some consequence, I begin to know the value of money better than I us'd to do. They dont wear very large ruffles. I hope to hear in your next that my Father is quite recover'd of the pain in his knee, I had about a week ago a curious pain in my knee, but I don't imagine it was the Gout, it plagu'd me for two days & then went off, it us'd to stun at times & as I had heard my Father talk of White swellings I began to be rather fright-n'd, but I was soon better so I thought no more of White swellings.

Mr. White is a sad madcaps, he never knows what he is about he has only spent about 15 or 20£ since he came & God knows how for he does not know himself. I have scarce room to send my Duty to you both & Love to all my good friends at Kellet including my two Cousins I am

Your most dutiful son

H. Ainslie

Cambridge *Novr. 3d 1777*

Monty never has had any old shirts, he has all that he brought with him.

The second letter, which is incomplete and lacks a date, was written at the end of his undergraduate career. It throws an interesting light on his reactions and those of the College, to his great success in the Tripos.

2 FROM HENRY AINSLIE TO HIS FATHER

Hond Father,

I receiv'd your kind letter this afternoon with two bills inclos'd, from my Brother & shall now for the last time from Cambridge write you a long letter, & in ye first place we will finish all College business. I told you in my last, & you will have seen in ye papers that I have got £25 for a prize, or at least shall get, immediately after Lady Day, but not before. I shall now tell you how I stand affected

1 Joseph Turner, Tutor of Pembroke, Senior Wrangler in 1767, became Master in 1784.

2 Richard Watson, Regius Professor of Divinity.

3 George Pretyman (1750–1827), Pembroke College, afterwards Sir George Pretyman Tomline, Bart. Senior Wrangler and first Smith's Prizeman in 1772. Elected Fellow 1773, Tutor 1776. (See also p. 99.)

4 James Brown, Master 1770–84.

5 William Pitt, entered the College in 1773.

with regard to the Fellows. Prytiman[1] is so much my friend, that I shou'd be asham'd even to doubt of his warm support; indeed I am more oblig'd to him than I can express for his assistance upon all occasions, & especially at degree time; he was my firm bulwark against the whole herd of private Tutors, who wou'd have made a trifle of me had they had it in their power, tho they all allow'd that I was clearly the best; but Milner[2] would have battled for ever for Law[3], had not Prytiman prevented him by swearing he wou'd never sign the Tripos, if I was not first[4]; the dispute then ran between Mont[5] & Law, Prytiman supported him to ye last but cou'd not get him first tho I am convinc'd he deserv'd it; & it appears more clearly by my Brothers having one vote & Law none, for one of ye Prizes; it was ye Bishop of Petersburghs[6]. Next for ye Master[7], who enquir'd for me every morning for this week past to breakfast with him, & wou'd never disturb me because I was not up; which as soon as I knew I got up to Chapel; & breakfasted with him; he told me he had enquir'd often for me; & was glad at last that he could see me; & in short behav'd so civilly to me that I am certain I am a great favourite; he told me I shou'd leave Cambridge with honour, that I had satisfied ye College in every particular, & that he had no doubt but that I shou'd proceed in ye same course & be a credit to my friends. Now for Turner[8] who the last is not of ye least consequence, I have seen him at different times since degree & I shall give you collectively the substance of all our Conversations & first, never man was so delighted (except yourself) when he heard I was first he shook my hand for 10 minutes & paid me a thousand Compliments, a few days after he call'd upon me, & told me I had done myself great credit, & had giv'n great pleasure to ye College & done it honor & yesterday he told me that if the St Bees Fellowship fell vacant, the College would be happy to elect me into it, & that if it did not, I had an equal chance with any other, & that he had not the least doubt but I wou'd be elected as soon as ever a Fellowship was vacant, which he said was rather a distant prospect, tho it appear'd a sure one; for that I had always behav'd well, was perfectly regular and a favourite with all the fellows. So far for him now for my own thoughts. There are two Fellowships now vacant to be fill'd next October by ye first & last Wranglers of last year[9]. The year after I shall be the only candidate who has any chance & mine will be a certainty if there is a vacancy, if not, I must wait till there is, & the first that falls I shall undoubtedly have. If nothing intervenes one of our Fellows will marry in about 13 Months, so that will just do, but this few people know but myself. In all likelyhood, one old incumbent at least may die in ye interim as some of our livings have men as old as ninety upon them, but be it as it may I think you will see that no fault of mine can prevent my election, & that

Figure 80 Joseph Turner (1745–1828). Tutor;
Master, 1784–1828. On the table are the *Life of
William Pitt* and *Works of Thomas Gray*.
Portrait by George Dawe, 1828.

1 Pretyman was Moderator in 1781, the year Ainslie took the Tripos: see above.

2 Isaac Milner, Queens' College, Moderator in the Tripos of 1780, afterwards President of Queens', Dean of Carlisle, Jacksonian Professor and Lucasian Professor.

3 George Henry Law, Queens' College, 1st Chancellor's Medal, afterwards Bishop of Chester and of Bath and Wells.

4 According to Gunning (*Reminiscences*, 2nd ed., vol. 1, p. 234) it was strongly felt in some quarters in the University that the 4th Wrangler, Thomas Catton of St John's, to whom the 1st Smith's Prize was awarded, should have been Senior Wrangler and charges of partiality were brought against private tutors.

5 Montague Farrer Ainslie, Henry's brother.

6 John Hinchcliffe, Master of Trinity 1768–88. Bishop of Peterborough 1769–94. An *ex-officio* examiner for the Smith's Prizes.

7 James Brown.

8 Joseph Turner (see above).

9 The Senior Wrangler of 1780 was St John Priest of Pembroke. He never became a Fellow. The last Wrangler (14th) was Francis Haggitt who was elected to a Fellowship at the same time as Henry Ainslie.

10 Henry Ainslie was elected Fellow on 30 October 1780.

nothing but the most rascally ill luck can hinder me from subscribing myself Fellow of Pem next October twelvemonth[10]. Turner desired me not to mention what he told me, he never gave the least hint to any person before, not even to Priest who was first last year. Now for London &c. As I shall ever take your advice with pleasure, I beg you will give it me whenever you think it necessary. I know ye principle which directs you, & I promise you I will attend to whatever you desire. I hope you will have no reason to be dissatisfied with my conduct in London any more than in Cambridge; the experience I have had here, has prepared me for more dangerous scenes, & I think I can oppose myself to all vice with firmness & success. I must confess my pride was hurt at ye prospect of living in obscurity in Town, & tho I wish not to be extravagant, yet I can never bear to live different to what I have done here; the difference in ye expence I have heard you say is only £10 a year to be a gentleman or blackguard; my Cousin Lind wishes to keep the £10 for you, & will doubtless advise you to keep me as cheap as possible this I have no objection to, it is what I wish; but not to be kept cheaper than possible. Mr Postlethwaite was astonish'd when I mention'd my having lodgings provided for me at £28 a year board & all, he said it was impossible for anybody to afford it & give me wholesome meat to eat, & advis'd me to seek out a lodging in some of ye little Inns of Court, Barnards or Furnivals, where they were cheap & good; I have heard…

6 THE VICTORIAN COLLEGE

The gentle pace of life in Pembroke in the eighteenth century, noted in the previous chapter, continued well into the nineteenth. Joseph Turner, elected Master in 1784, held office for over 43 years; Gilbert Ainslie, his successor, for over 41. Ainslie was devoted to the College and in the early years of his Mastership was active in extending the College site. The average entry at this time was about fifteen and these included two who were to be counted among Pembroke's greatest intellects, the scientist George Gabriel Stokes and the lawyer Henry Maine. By the middle of the century, however, the entry had dropped to an average of less than nine; in 1858 the one man admitted left for Caius after five days. Another brilliant scientist, John Couch Adams, was elected to the fellowship at about this time but, as an undergraduate of those days later wrote, 'Nowhere in the world, save perhaps in the heart of China, would you light upon so delightful, peaceful, drowsy, comfortable, venerable, useless a caravanserai of idleness. Such institutions in our midst are relics of a dead and gone civilization.' Ainslie died in 1870, by which time matters had begun to improve slightly. It was, however, in the next decade, under his successor John Power, that the College embarked upon one of its most ambitious and drastic phases of expansion.

The Victorian buildings

In the early nineteenth century, with about ten fellows and a few undergraduates in residence, there was no need for new buildings. Up until the 1870s the College remained very much as it had been in 1670 and consisted largely of Old Court, Ivy Court and the Wren Chapel. Gilbert Ainslie (figure 81), a tireless antiquary who pored over the College records and wrote elaborate accounts of College history, showed remarkable disregard for the College buildings. When Robert Willis was making investigations for his *Architectural history of the University of Cambridge*, Ainslie wrote to him in 1854: 'Excepting our Chapel there is nothing to interest anyone, and, unless that be

Figure 81 Gilbert Ainslie (1793–1870), the son of Henry Ainslie (see. p. 102); Master (1828–1870) and twice Vice-Chancellor. Artist unknown; the portrait appears to be based on a photograph of Ainslie.

spared, all will probably be rased in 20 or 30 years from this time.' His gloomy prophecy was to prove uncannily accurate. Ainslie, however, saw that as the centre of Cambridge was being built over, it was important to add to the College site for future expansion and here he was energetic and successful (see p. 16).

In 1776 William Mason and the Master, James Brown had each given £50 in memory of their friend Thomas Gray, and Mason wished that the money 'shou'd not be applied to any slight or accidental repair of the College', but invested 'till such time as the Society shall find it expedient to rebuild one whole side of either of the Quadrangles or a new building next the Garden'. Thus began the Building Fund, which was much augmented by a major bequest received in 1807. This came from Mrs Sara Lonsdale of Barham Hall. She had been the wife first of Robert Millicent of Barham and then of Christopher Lonsdale, a former Tutor of Peterhouse. In honour of William Pitt she decided to leave to Pembroke her estate at Barham, near Linton, Cambridgeshire, directing that the income from one

Figure 82 The medieval Hall, after Cory's renovations of 1862. Two tables suffice for the undergraduates; propped against one and providing an appropriately 'medieval' touch is a bizarre, probably nineteenth-century musical instrument, a ' harp-lute', still in the College's possession. Cory's gasoliers and tiles are authentically Victorian. The panelling and the carving above the fireplace, both dating from 1634, are now at the high-table end of the Hall. Photograph of about 1870.

third of it should be added to the Building Fund. In the early 1800s the Lonsdale bequest produced an average of about £100 a year; by 1850 this had risen to about £400 a year. (The annual Barham Dinner, for junior members about to graduate or complete their postgraduate work, commemorates this bequest.)

By mid-century, a Royal Commission was beginning to examine the workings of the University and make reforms. Colleges were fearful that large unused balances might be appropriated to University needs. The Building Fund, which had accumulated to nearly £100,000, was thought to be especially at risk. Pembroke's first moves to use it were conservative and relatively inexpensive: it was decided to renovate the old Hall. The architect chosen was John Cory, of Carlisle, whose brother Alexander Cory had been a Fellow of Pembroke (1839–56). Cory's work (completed 1862) was generally approved by antiquaries and historians. The exterior of the Hall was re-Gothicised, the old windows remodelled and the classical doorcase (see p. 20) removed. Inside, Cory designed a new oak ceiling, based on fragments which he found concealed behind panelling in the gallery. Less archaeologically correct were the rich encaustic floor tiles and the ornate brass gasoliers which he introduced (figure 82).

In 1870 when John Power (figure 83) became Master the mood changed almost at once, from quiet conservatism to almost frenetic zeal for development. Undergraduate numbers were increasing – from 43 when Power became Master to 122 when he died ten years later. The College buildings were seen as cramped and difficult to extend. Now was the time to use the still substantial resources of the Building Fund.

Figure 83 John Power (1818–80), Master, 1870–80, by W. Vizard.

Figure 84 Alfred Waterhouse (1830–1905). Portrait by Sir Lawrence Alma-Tadema, in the National Portrait Gallery.

A fashionable architect was needed, rather than the provincial Cory, and the College's choice fell on Alfred Waterhouse (figure 84), who had already done much college work in Oxford and Cambridge, including a bold and ambitious new building for Caius. Waterhouse was asked to suggest 'the best way of providing for the College a group of buildings, as efficient, convenient and architecturally effective as the site was capable of'. His plan envisaged the rebuilding of the entire college. Not even Wren's Chapel would have been spared: its removal would have been 'a matter of regret', but it would give Waterhouse the chance to build an Italianate campanile 'sufficiently high to be the most conspicuous tower in Cambridge, which suffers from the lack of lofty architectural features'. (In fact, the assertive Congregational church tower across Trumpington Street was to provide the feature which Waterhouse desired.)

The Fellows preferred a more cautious, phased approach. Waterhouse first designed a new range of rooms, Red Buildings (1871–2), on Crossinge's Place. This was not controversial, since the site had not formed part of the medieval college. The result, however, was startling: an aggressive red-brick building with a high tower, in French Renaissance style (figure 85), a style completely new to Cambridge. Next, John Power wished for a new Master's Lodge, removed from the old college buildings, and Waterhouse designed a quieter red-brick villa, in a heavy Gothic style, on the site of Paschal's Yard (1873).

This too was unobjectionable, but then the changes started to eat away the historic fabric of the College. The old Master's Lodge (p. 81) was demolished in 1874. At the same time the south range of Old Court was removed, opening up a vista to the Chapel but destroying for ever the intimate (or constricted) scale of Old Court, as set out in the fourteenth century. Once the Lodge and the south range were gone, the Hall looked ramshackle. Some, including Waterhouse, argued that its stability, undermined when Cory extended the cellars under it in the 1860s, was now imperilled by the removal of buildings which had buttressed it. Waterhouse was first asked to extend the old Hall, but his design has not survived. Late in 1874 Waterhouse told the Fellows that he 'would be glad' if they would consent to at least partial demolition. The Fellows, though startled by this sudden demand, could see little alternative to demolishing the Hall completely, and early in 1875 they agreed.

When news of the threat to the medieval Hall broke, there was a furious campaign by old members to save it, conducted in the newspapers or by letter. They objected to the destruction of 'a group of buildings of so picturesque a character, of such architectural value, and of such great antiquity'. To sweep such buildings away was 'wilfully to tear a page out of the architectural history of our University'.

Figure 85 Red Buildings. Drawing by
Waterhouse of the elevation towards the College.

Waterhouse, in a letter to *The Times* in March 1875, was dismissive of the
old Hall and Cory's work: 'imitation 14th century windows. . . a new
ceiling and floor. . . in all probability, nothing now remains of the original structure than portions of the core of the walls, formed. . . of
clunch rubble work, which, when opened out, have proved to be without bond or cohesion'. Typical of the objectors' views were those of
Edmund Venables, Precentor of Lincoln, who thought that Cory's
'faithfulness to the original features of the building deserves the high-
est commendation': he had recreated 'one of the most exquisitely
beautiful designs of the medieval domestic architecture'. The Fellows,
however, were unmoved. Charles Octavus Budd, Senior Fellow,
summed up their feelings in his letter to *The Times* when, while com-
mending Cory's work, he felt that 'he put so respectable a face on
things that people erroneously imagined such repairs and alterations
were still possible, while the younger generation has regarded his wood
decoration of the interior of the hall as a relic of antiquity to be religiously preserved'. So, in a tersely worded minute of 16 March 1875 the
Fellows recorded: 'It was agreed that Mr. Waterhouse be authorised to
pull down the College Hall.' The Tutor, Charles Searle, later to be
Master, did not sign the order, an indication, perhaps, that the Fellows'
unanimity about the redevelopment scheme was breaking down.

The hall

Small – for her house was modest – and yet fair
  The refectory which our Lady plann'd;
  And half a thousand years her scholars there
  Ate and gave thanks – Lyndwood and all that band
  Of statesman prelates. Overhead did stand
  The library, with chambers higher still,
  Built by a Chancellor's enlighten'd hand,
  First of five Masters[1] York's high throne to fill.

  The College grew. Money for Gray's sake given,
  Pitt helping, mounted up to build. At last
  A Quaker saint, as architect call'd in,
  Hall, library, and half the house – just Heaven!
  From the foundations Mary laid did blast.
What is the punishment when good men sin?

from A. J. Mason: *Pembroke Sonnets*

1 Lawrence Booth, Thomas Rotherham, Edmund Grindall, Matthew Hutton and Samuel Harsnett.

Waterhouse's new Hall (1875–6) was much larger than the old and reverted to the original arrangement of a single room with an open timber roof. To the south, where the old Lodge had stood, Waterhouse added a range with combination room on the ground floor and chambers above, reached by stairs in a turret crowned with a conical cap (figure 86). Over the roof was a lantern. To the south again, across the lawn from the new Hall, Waterhouse now designed a new Library (1877–8) in a continental Gothic style, with a Belgian-style clock tower (figures 87, 88). From the entrance to the College the view of the new Library, seen between Wren's Chapel and Waterhouse's Hall, was (and still is) undeniably picturesque.

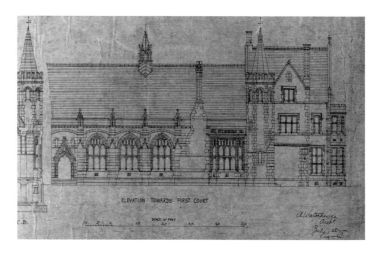

Figure 86 The Hall. Elevation towards First Court, signed by Waterhouse and dated 1875. This shows the Hall as built, before the drastic alterations of 1926.

Figure 87 The Library, from First Court. The spire on the clock-tower formerly echoed the lantern and the cap on the stair turret of the Hall as originally built by Waterhouse.

Figure 88 Library interior, looking west. The dignity of this room, still very much as left by Waterhouse, is worth setting against the sometimes harshly assertive qualities of his exteriors.

Not much of the medieval college now remained and Waterhouse and John Power were keen to complete the remodelling; but the controversy about the old Hall led the Fellows to reconsider whether Waterhouse had been the right choice. However, in 1878 they voted to destroy the now disused Library, with its fine plaster ceiling (figure 57); but they voted also to dismiss Waterhouse. At a College Meeting the merits of several architects, G. F. Bodley, Richard Norman Shaw, Arthur Blomfield, Basil Champneys, as well as Cory and Waterhouse, were considered before the choice fell on George Gilbert Scott, son of the famous Gothicist Sir Gilbert Scott, and an architect well known for a cautious approach to restoration. The Treasurer, C.H. Prior, was deputed to write to Waterhouse: 'Having resolved to keep the old buildings we think it best to apply to someone whose style is specially conservative.' The charge that he had failed to be 'conservative enough' upset Waterhouse greatly.

Figure 89 Chapel interior, showing Scott's
masterly extension of the east end with
coupled Corinthian columns between
sanctuary and nave.

Figure 90 New Court.

Scott's brief was to consider the Trumpington Street front, the Chapel and the Old Library, and to plan a new building in the northeast corner of the site. By 1879 he was telling the College, 'I have no doubt at all that what remains of the ancient buildings of the College should be religiously preserved.' Scott delayed submitting plans for the remodelling of the Old Library in the hope that the College would reconsider its earlier decision. 'I do not wish to have the discredit of having destroyed a fine old room', he wrote in April 1880. Shortly afterwards the College voted to reverse its earlier decision and to restore the Old Library as a meeting room.

Scott provided much-needed additional space in the Chapel by extending it in a sympathetic style, moving the east wall eastwards by one bay and marking the division between old and new work with a bold triumphal arch with massive coupled Corinthian columns of Italian marble from Saravezza in the Apennines (figure 89). The arch was derived from one designed by Wren for St. Paul's Cathedral. His suggestion that the plaster wall panels and ceiling of the chapel should

Figure 91 New Court. Newel posts such as this occur on all staircases and are typical of Scott's detailing.

be painted and gilded was not adopted. Some decoration was provided in 1906 when Mrs. Laurence Humphry, daughter of Sir George Gabriel Stokes, provided a stained glass window in memory of her father. The window, Flemish in style, depicting College benefactors surrounding the Crucifixion, was designed by her brother-in-law G.W. Humphry and executed by Burlison and Grylls.

Still more accommodation was needed and in 1881 Scott built New Court (figure 90), a striking stone building on the site of the old Tennis Court, in a style combining features of 16th-, 17th- and 18th-century architecture, and with almost Arts and Crafts motifs in the groups of angels sculpted at the exterior corners and in some of the interior woodwork (figure 91). Along the string course above the first floor a series of shields carried letters spelling out the text 'Nisi Dominus aedificat domum ...' (Except the Lord build the house, their labour is but vain that build it.)

Peter Meadows

Figure 92 Thomas Barnes.

Journalism, Law, the Church, Science: some nineteenth-century Pembroke men

THOMAS BARNES (1785–1841)

Barnes was editor of *The Times* from 1817 to 1841, an important figure both in the history of that newspaper and in the political and national life of the time. He was at Pembroke 1804–08. The portrait (now lost) was copied from the picture now in the National Portrait Gallery, 'Caroline of Brunswick, Queen consort of George IV before the House of Lords, August 1820, during discussion of the bill to dissolve her marriage', in which Barnes is among the spectators.

SIR HENRY SUMNER MAINE (1822–1888)

A brilliant classicist as undergraduate at Pembroke, Maine is celebrated as an academic lawyer who urged the importance of history for a proper understanding of law. His most famous work, *Ancient Law* (1861), published two years after Darwin's *Origin of Species* and reflecting the contemporary interest in evolution, argued that all societies exhibit similar stages of legal development. Others had previously speculated in similar terms but Maine pointed to the lack of empirical research and urged close study of the records of ancient peoples and of surviving primitive communities.

For Maine the earliest stage of legal development, the stage visible in the Homeric poems, was one in which kings uttered divinely inspired judgments about particular disputes. In the next stage, such judgments were consolidated into custom, superintended by the oligarchies which succeeded the kings. The more democratic third stage saw the adoption of codes, such as the Twelve Tables of Rome. 'Dynamic' societies could then progress even further, employing the different techniques of change constituted by fictions, equity, and legislation. Maine's most celebrated insight was his view that dynamic or 'progressive' societies were all marked by the gradual dissolution of dependency on the family and the growth of individual obligation as their primary characteristic: 'All the forms of Status taken notice of in the Law of Persons were derived from, and to some extent are still coloured by, the powers and privileges anciently residing in the Family. If then we employ Status . . . to signify these personal conditions only . . . we may say that the movement of the progressive societies has hitherto been a movement from Status to Contract.' (*Ancient Law*, pp. 173–4.)

Maine became a Fellow of Trinity Hall soon after graduating. In 1847 he was appointed Regius Professor of Civil Law in Cambridge and in 1852 became the first reader in Roman law and jurisprudence to

Figure 93 Henry Sumner Maine. Artist's replica of the portrait by Lowes C. Dickinson at Trinity Hall (1890).

be appointed by the Inns of Court in their initial attempt to stimulate legal education. In 1862 Maine accepted appointment as legal member of the Council of the Viceroy of India, in which office he advised the Indian government on a wide range of legal and political issues.

After his appointment to the newly founded Corpus chair of jurisprudence at Oxford (1869) Maine published a number of books that pursued the work begun in *Ancient Law: Village Communities in the East and the West* (1871), *Early history of institutions* (1875), *Early law and custom* (1883). He became Master of Trinity Hall in 1877 and was elected an Honorary Fellow of Pembroke in 1887, the year in which he became Whewell Professor of International Law. An able journalist, Maine often published articles on political and economic issues, and the appearance of his volume of essays on *Popular Government* in 1885, in which he warned of the defects of democracy, stirred controversy. Observing that all that had made England famous and wealthy had been the work of minorities, 'sometimes very small ones', he concluded that 'we may say generally that the gradual establishment of the masses in power is the blackest omen for all legislation founded on scientific opinion, which requires tension of mind to understand it, and self-denial to submit to it'.

Trevor Allan

Figure 94 Thomas Fanshaw Middleton. Detail from the engraving by H. Meyer from a drawing (also in the College's possession) by J. Jackson.

Figure 95 Neptune. Photograph by NASA.

TWO COLONIAL BISHOPS

Thomas Fanshaw Middleton (1769–1822) came up to Pembroke from Christ's Hospital, where he was a school-fellow of S.T. Coleridge and Charles Lamb. He graduated in 1792 and was ordained in the same year. While a Lincolnshire curate he edited and in great part wrote a short-lived periodical, *The Country Spectator*. He was a notable scholar and his book, *The doctrine of the Greek article applied to the criticism and the illustration of the New Testament* (1808) went through five editions. He was made Bishop of Calcutta in 1814, in which role he saw his main task as being to minister to the European community, rather than to attempt the conversion of the local population.

William Grant Broughton (1788–1853) entered Pembroke some years after leaving school. He graduated and was ordained in 1818. He rose in the church and in 1828 was appointed to the chaplaincy of the Tower of London. The following year he became Archdeacon of New South Wales. There was at that time no Anglican bishop in Australia and his jurisdiction extended over the whole of Australia and the adjoining islands. The same situation obtained when in 1836 Broughton was made Bishop of Australia. His vast see was subdivided only in 1847, when he became Bishop of Sydney and Metropolitan of Australasia.

TWO SCIENTISTS

John Couch Adams came to Pembroke as a Fellow in 1853, from St John's. The discovery of the planet Neptune in 1846 following the predictions of Adams, and independently of U. J. J. Le Verrier, is one of the great exploits of nineteenth-century deductive science. Uranus, the outermost of the then known planets, had completed about three-quarters of its 84-year orbit since its discovery in 1781 and it had become clear that its motion was inconsistent with that expected from the gravitational pull of the Sun and known planets. In 1843 Adams, after completing his BA, acted on the growing speculation that a further planet was causing the discrepancy by calculating where and how big the planet should be. In 1845 he sent his predictions to the University Observatories, but verification was hampered by poor weather and lack of good star charts. Work was still in progress when news came from Berlin of the discovery of the planet, essentially as Adams had predicted, following parallel but independent calculations by Le Verrier in Paris.

George Gabriel Stokes was one of the great mathematical physicists of the nineteenth century. Born in 1819 in County Sligo, he came to Pembroke in 1837, was a Fellow from 1841 until his marriage in 1857 and again, after Fellows were allowed to be married, from 1869

Figure 96 John Couch Adams. Portrait by
Hubert Herkomer, 1888.

Figure 97 George Gabriel Stokes. Photograph by Mrs F. W. H. Myers, 1892.

until becoming Master a few months before his death in 1903. He held the Lucasian Professorship from 1849 and was for a while also President of the Royal Society and Member of Parliament for the University, a combination of offices shared only by Newton.

His name occurs in all A-level and undergraduate physics courses, in three different contexts stemming from work done in the early 1850s:

1850: Stokes' formula $6\pi\eta av$ for the drag force on a sphere of radius a travelling with velocity v in a medium of viscosity η. This is merely the most memorable result in a 99-page paper exploring the dynamics of viscous flow. It is typical of Stokes' many-sidedness that this fundamental research was actuated by one of the severest practical problems of the day, that of accurate time-keeping: how does the air-drag on a pendulum affect the accuracy of a clock?

1852: Stokes' parameters, now denoted I, Q, U and V, for quantifying the state of polarisation of arbitrarily polarised light. They have the simple property that when light comes from two independent sources the Stokes' parameters of the combined beam are just the sums of those from the two sources separately.

1854: Stokes' theorem in differential geometry, commonly quoted in Gibbs vector notation as:

$$\int \mathbf{F} \cdot \mathbf{ds} = \int \operatorname{curl} \mathbf{F} \cdot \mathbf{dS}.$$

Stokes was examiner for the Smith's Prize and set the proof of this result as one of the questions. His name became attached to the equation, though in fact its discovery belongs to his great Peterhouse contemporary William Thomson (Lord Kelvin).

These are cited as the three most easily stateable and best known results in an immense body of work in mathematics and physics, for which over the years Stokes was feted with honours and distinctions. The 50th anniversary in 1899 of Stokes' election to the Lucasian Professorship of Mathematics was attended by impressive celebrations. Delegates from universities all over the world attended ceremonies in the Senate House, a dinner at Trinity College and a reception in Pembroke, the attendance at which must be easily the most distinguished body of people that has ever assembled on the College site (figure 98). Stokes was eighty years old at the time: he was to live until 1903.

Sidney Kenderdine

Figure 98 Photograph of some of those attending Stokes' jubilee celebrations. Stokes is seated in the middle of the front row, under the centre of the arch. The photograph shows the present Hall as originally designed by Waterhouse.

Sir George Stokes

Not much he spoke. Far off beyond the ken
  Of other thinkers ranged his thought. A smile
  Of courteous patience touch'd his features while
  He lent an ear to ordinary men.
  Yet all the duties of a citizen
  Claim'd him. He sat where Newton sat before,
  Our burgess; and for science long he bore
  The labour of the secretary's pen.

  The assembled world brought homage to his chair.
  And this man held it sure that none but they
  Have endless life, who know the Son of God.
  "Tell the young men to walk," his last words were,
  "In holiness; it is the only way."
Full fourscore years himself that way had trod.

from A. J. Mason: *Pembroke Sonnets*

The beginning of the College Mission

In 1885 the Great Depression was at its worst while in the Church and in Cambridge the evangelical revival and the social movement were running strong. On 5 March of that year a visitor from Toynbee Hall, the Universities' Settlement in Whitechapel, spoke to undergraduates in the Old Reader. Sin might result from poverty rather than poverty from sin. An Open Meeting of undergraduates and resident BAs was called for 12 March. Should the College commit itself to Toynbee Hall and to Whitechapel, or should it act independently? A committee of four was appointed to inquire. Approaches to old members produced pledges of £108 annually for three years for a College venture, £5,100 p.a. in today's money. The Bishop of Rochester was urging parochial missions to move across the river into South London. Accordingly, after stopping at Toynbee Hall and at one or two of the public school missions, the committee crossed London Bridge into the country's largest area of unbroken poverty, where 'Christianity was not in possession'. In a sermon preached in Chapel early in the Easter term another great evangelistic Bishop, Walsham How, hinted that need might indeed be greater across the Thames. On 29 April an emissary from the Bishop of Rochester met with a great welcome in the Old Reader; this was C. H. Grundy, Wilberforce Missioner for South London, thereafter a regular favourite with undergraduates. Within twenty-four hours a crowded Open Meeting had resolved four to one in favour of starting an independent College Mission.

The district which the Bishop of Rochester offered lay half a mile south east of the Elephant and Castle, in the parish of All Saints, Newington, an exceptionally populous area in the heart of Walworth. Here five thousand souls were crowded into twelve acres, an area scarcely twice the size of the College site. There were seven public houses, a school on Flint Street which still stands, a police station on Rodney Road, a wheelwright's shop and, at one end of Barlow Street, a common lodging house for the down and out. The local aristocracy were employed as porters at the Bricklayers' Arms Depot, or as printers, smiths, and tradesmen. The rest were costermongers, carmen and casual labourers; their children matchboys or newsboys, or worse, along Fleet Street and the Strand. The men's weekly wage might be eight shillings, of which the rent took one third. The stretch of Huntsman Street between Halpin Place and Barlow Street, where the Pembroke House building has now stood for over a century, was plumb in the middle of the district which Bishop Thorold offered.

The Open Meeting's resolution was promptly put into effect. On 27 May 1885 the Mission held its first general meeting, upstairs in the

College Library. The Master, C. E. Searle, was in the chair but of all the senior members involved in the start of the Mission none seems more important than Charles Herman Prior, a migrant from Caius, who was to become Tutor in 1890, and was to see the venture through its first decade. The Bishop's offer of the Barlow Street district was formally accepted. Rules were passed which, with a small early change, continued on the books until recently. The committee of four thereupon bowed out and was replaced by an executive of fourteen, later increased to twenty. Finding a missioner and a Mission hall occupied the first few months. In the Old Library on 14 November, in one of his bright and earnest speeches, Bishop Thorold himself introduced to the College their first Missioner, Montague Charles Sturges. A graduate and then chaplain of that short-lived Cambridge foundation of Cavendish Hall, Sturges had been a curate at Godstone in the diocese of Rochester. He was to spend most of his pastoral life in South London. He was Missioner to 1889, living for the first year just off the Walworth Road at 36 Wansey Street and thereafter at 207A East Street, in what became known as the Pembroke house.

When the general committee next met, early in February 1886, the first Mission hall had been found and a lease taken for £50 a year. A stone's throw from the present building, 79 Elsted Street was at the time the largest room in the district save for the wheelwright's shop. The building was a disused broom factory, which had served its turn as skittle alley and rope walk. It seated 160. It was there that at 11 a.m. on Sunday, 28 March 1886, with a choir and a congregation of ninety children, the Mission was inaugurated. The following Friday there was a service for Pembroke men; the address was given by H. W. Webb-Peploe, Vicar of St Paul's, Onslow Square, a notable evangelical preacher and father of a first-year undergraduate.

The undergraduates and BAs who had started the Mission and who, on that 2nd April, might have been in the congregation, were mostly merchants' sons, from public schools whose own missions had been going for a decade or more. With few exceptions they went on to ordination. The Pembroke College Debating Society ran the Junior Parlour in those days and, although there is no suggestion of a formal link, the names of its officers recur among those active in the new creation. There would be some 'blues' among them, including the first Pembroke president of the CUBC, E. Lambert. From the earliest Henley crews there was A. F. Sim, who became a missionary in Nyasaland and succumbed to the climate there in 1895; and W. A. Hunter, the first Pembroke Missioner in Walworth (1889), who succeeded Sturges and died of illness after scarcely a year on the job – a sincere and witty man, representative of those who come to life in the minutes of the PCDS. G. L. Pilkington was to be an

African missionary too; he translated the Bible into Lugandan, and lost his life at the storming of Lubwa's Fort during the Ugandan wars of religion in 1897. From the committee of four J. H. Greig became Wilberforce Missioner after Grundy, and then Vicar of St Paul's, Lorrimore Square, half a mile from the Mission, before going on to build Guildford Cathedral when he was Bishop.

One hundred years on the Mission still stands, almost alone among these Oxbridge good works. The fashions of the sixties and seventies were against anything patronising: missions were closed or handed over. The fashions of the nineties have revived the virtue of the 'inner city', where often the Church has alone stayed. Pembroke House, as it became in 1952, has been rejigged as needs and enthusiasms change. But the church, now called St Christopher's, has been restored to the heart of the buildings. The Missioner, paid by the diocese, is now the vicar of a distinct parish. The Walworth youngsters tax the inventiveness of youth workers funded by borough and charity. And Pembroke College men and women still subscribe, visit, live for a year in the House, and entertain pensioners to bowls on the College green.

Adapted from an article by Michael Kuczynski in *PCCS Annual Gazette*, **59** (1985); the final paragraph by Brian Watchorn.

College servants

Were I historian, lief would I ensure
    That Stoakley's fame, and Chapman's,[1] should abide,
    With other men and women train'd and tried
    In College service. May their names endure
    In grateful admiration! Tasks obscure,
    Done well, themselves are noble, and provide
    That leisure which our Lady will'd to guide[2]
    The quest of science and good literature.

    Men tell us that beneath the Southern seas
    Small lives unnumber'd have been spent in toil,
    Not knowing why, till from the brine there hove
    The isle of coral, and a fertile soil,
    Where stately palms bask in the fragrant breeze
And birds of gorgeous feather flit from grove to grove.

from A. J. Mason: *Pembroke Sonnets*

1 J. T. Stoakley was elected Under Porter in 1854, and Head Porter in 1892. Arthur Chapman's connection with the College began in 1876; in 1895 he was appointed Butler, and in 1903 Manager of Kitchens and Buttery.
2 The Foundress made provision for a Master or Keeper, six Fellows, two Bible Clerks 'and the requisite Servants', of whom the 'Famulus Custodis' was one.

Silver by Paul Storr

Paul Storr (1771–1844) was the leading English Regency silversmith. The College has a notable collection of his work.

Figure 99 Tankard and cover by Paul Storr, decorated with Tudor roses and shell motifs in two bands and with a shell thumbpiece (1809). McQuade Bequest.

Figure 100 Three boxes by Paul Storr decorated with allegorical scenes. The largest portrays Diana, Victory, Bacchus and King Midas, seated on clouds, at a banquet. The scenes on the two smaller boxes are related: one shows Phaethon entreating permission to drive the chariot of his father, the Sun; the other shows his subsequent failure and the metamorphosis of his sisters (who had harnessed the horses for him) into trees – a punishment inflicted by Jupiter.

Silver-gilt. 1830/31 (i.e. towards the end of Storr's career). The circular rim bases bear a mark of 1845 and were added later, but in his workshop. The gift of Edward Willan (Pembroke 1935–38) in 1993.

7 THE TWENTIETH CENTURY

In an era of national expansion in higher education, Pembroke has seen in this century building work at least equal in extent to that of the Victorian period, beginning with Pitt Building and culminating in the new building, which has brought a 50% increase in student accommodation on the College site. This is, however, less than many other Cambridge colleges have done and the same may be said of student numbers. For the first half of the century, with an annual undergraduate entry (apart from the war years) of around a hundred, Pembroke was one of the larger colleges. Subsequently it has been overtaken, since other colleges have increased their intake while Pembroke's has remained more or less static: it is now one of the smaller colleges. Pembroke has, however, participated notably in the recent expansion in graduate student numbers in the University, so that the total junior member population (undergraduates and graduates) is at present 560. The size of the Fellowship, for many years static at around twenty, has increased markedly since about 1960 and is now over 60. The other major demographic change this century has been the admission of women to the College since 1983. Their numbers are currently approaching 40% of junior members and 15% of Fellows.

As the story of Pembroke is brought up to the present day the amount of available detail becomes dauntingly large and the hazards of selection proportionately great. If it is suggested that in this century Pembroke has been conspicuous academically for its contributions to mathematics and oriental studies, that is not to belittle a distinguished tradition of studies in English literature or R. R. Porter's Nobel Prize for his work on the chemistry of antibodies. Among many notable lawyers the name of Lord Taylor, Lord Chief Justice, will perhaps be particularly remembered. Pembroke has continued to produce poets in numbers disproportionate to its size, including the present Poet Laureate, and there have been notable composers, as well as performing musicians. Better known to the public at large than any of these has been the recent group of entertainers, among them Peter Cook.

Figure 101 Pitt Building from Ivy Court, with the seventeenth-century doorcase from the old Hall to the right.

Buildings

As first built, the Waterhouse Master's Lodge (p. 112; now the Old Master's Lodge or N staircase) was a free-standing building, with its main entrance on Pembroke Street from a spacious forecourt (now the Fellows' car-park). The Master's stables lay to the west of the Lodge. The Fellows' Garden stretched from the Lodge right across the College site to Tennis Court Terrace: to this undergraduates had no access and they could reach New Court only via Pembroke Street. This rather extraordinary state of affairs (as it would now seem) persisted until 1907, when the steady increase in student numbers necessitated further extensions. Scott, the College's most recent architect, had become insane by the mid-1880s and died in 1897. W. D. Caröe, architect to the Ecclesiastical Commissioners and best known as a designer of churches, was now brought in.

PITT BUILDING, O STAIRCASE AND THE BRIDGE

Caröe designed two buildings. The first, Pitt Building (M staircase), between Ivy Court and the Lodge, is a picturesque red-brick range in an Arts and Crafts style with much ingenious and carefully designed detail (figure 101). To the south, on the garden side, it presents a pleasing row of dormer windows under stone gables, reminiscent of those on the south side of Ivy Court (p. 57), while to the court it displays a lively array of brick chimneys and stone gables of various widths and angles. His second building is a modest extension of New Court (O staircase), in style identical to Scott's, which linked it to the Lodge. Caröe then completed the job by linking up his two buildings with what is perhaps his most striking addition: the arched stone screen along Pembroke Street (figure 102). This is an effective composition in a late Baroque style and greatly enhances the long street façade. It was not intended to be purely decorative, however: its principal function was to act as a bridge by which undergraduates, crossing the Master's forecourt at first-floor level from Pitt Building, could reach New Court without needing to leave College or trespass on the Fellows' Garden. (The present route through the garden to New Court was opened up only in the 1940s.)

THE HALL

By the mid-1920s the Fellows had become thoroughly disenchanted with Waterhouse's Hall. Sir Ellis Minns spoke for many when he criticised the open roof structure – 'the sensation was that of a crushing weight above one's head' – and the décor: 'Of the panelling and screens I have always wondered how such good material could have been used to produce so mean an effect'. In 1926 the College decided to repeat what had been done to the medieval Hall in the fifteenth century (p. 20), and remove the open roof, put in a flat ceiling and introduce two storeys of rooms above. All this was the work of Maurice Webb, son of the Edwardian baroque architect Sir Aston Webb. At the same time the wall between the Hall and the Fellows' combination room was taken down, the latter being made into a high-table dais. A new Senior Parlour was created on the ground floor of Hitcham Building. In 1949, with Murray Easton (who had recently designed the 1939–45 War Memorial (see p. 138)) as architect, the Gothic tracery of Waterhouse's windows was replaced by a simpler design, not dissimilar to that of the medieval Hall.

Figure 102 The bridge joining Pitt Building to New Court, from Pembroke Street. (Photograph taken c. 1908)

Figure 103 The 1933 Master's Lodge, by
Maurice Webb.

THE 1933 MASTER'S LODGE

The Waterhouse Master's Lodge was used for that purpose for only
about sixty years. It was then decided to build a new Lodge (the
College's third) remote from all other College buildings, on the
south-east corner of the site in the angle of Tennis Court Road and
Tennis Court Terrace. There was ample space here, which allowed
Maurice Webb to design a large three-storied neo-Georgian brick
villa (figure 103). The main entrance was once again off the street and
Fellows or undergraduates visiting the Master had to leave College
to gain access. Completed in 1933, the building was demolished in
1996 to allow construction of the new building.

ORCHARD BUILDING

Orchard building, so named because it stands on part of the
Foundress's orchard, was completed in 1957 to the design of Marshall
Sisson. This is a self-contained, three-storied block, neo-Georgian in
style and of conventional Cambridge collegiate design in that

Harry Frank Guggenheim (1890–1971), benefactor and Honorary Fellow, may be remembered at this point because among his many gifts to the College was one that contributed substantially to the cost of Orchard Building.

He attended the Columbia Grammar School in New York City and the Sheffield School at Yale to learn about metals; in Mexico he was apprenticed for three years in the smelter at Aguascalientes. When he came up to Pembroke in 1910 he was already married and had two children: he rented Leckhampton House. He entered enthusiastically into Cambridge life, played tennis for the University, was taught by J. M. Keynes and took his BA in 1913. In the First World War, as lieutenant commander, he flew with the US Navy in Italy and at St Mihiel. He backed Byrd's flight to the North Pole (1926), ran the family mining interests, and was Herbert Hoover's ambassador to Cuba between the wars. In the 1930s he promoted R. H. Goddard's work on rocket propulsion and later brought von Kármán to Caltech. He published an aeronautical memoir; with his wife he published on Long Island the world's largest suburban daily. A major philanthropist, in 1943 he commissioned Frank Lloyd Wright to build on 5th Avenue the Guggenheim Museum of Non-Objective Painting (opened 1959). On active service in the Pacific in the Second World War he was promoted captain and was on the escort carrier *Nehenta Bay* in the Okinawa campaign of May and June 1945. Horse racing was among his favourite hobbies and his *Dark Star* won the Kentucky Derby Stakes. The College's annual Guggenheim Dinner is funded by his 'donation to increase the amenities of the Society'.

accommodation is arranged around three staircases. Stylistically, this was one of the last backward-looking collegiate buildings in Cambridge. It does not, perhaps, make the best use of an important site and the junction with New Court, where the two buildings meet corner to corner, is awkwardly handled. The Gibbs surrounds of the doorways are the strongest element in the design of the facade and echo those of the ground-floor windows in New Court. The materials are of high quality: a buff-coloured Dutch brick, with cornice, string courses and doorways of Clipsham stone; the roof is of copper. There is a finely carved and painted coat of arms on the north end of the building.

A. V. Grimstone & Peter Meadows

THE NEW BUILDING

There were three distinct phases in the planning of the new court; a master plan for the College site; an aborted proposal for a new building that retained the 1933 Master's Lodge; and the development of the scheme as now built. The project took ten years of more or less continuous work, at varying levels of intensity, to complete. It spanned two Masterships at Pembroke and three at Peterhouse, who sold the land in question to Pembroke in 1861 (p. 16) with a number of restrictive covenants that had to be observed. As with most building projects, three principal groups have been involved, the client, the design team and the contractors. The pace of the development has been slower than usual but in the light of Pembroke's six and a half centuries, so bound up with its setting and buildings, a decade is insignificant. The great care and responsibility shown for the quality of environment by the College's Buildings Committee is in my experience (unhappily) unusual.

In 1987 my practice (EP Associates Ltd) was chosen to develop a master plan to allow the College to increase the number of students living on site and additionally to locate a replacement space for the Old Reader, needed to allow expansion of the College library. In preparation for this we undertook a reconstruction of the development of the College fabric from its foundation to modern times (figure 104) and traced the changing character and uses of the gardens and buildings. The conclusion of this study was that the large area to the south of the avenue, occupied at that time by the Master's Lodge and the Master's and Fellows' Gardens, clearly provided the greatest potential for development with the least disturbance to the rest of the College. A site – bounded by Red Buildings, the Chapel and the Library – was also identified where an underground auditorium might one day be built.

Figure 104 The development of College buildings over six and a half centuries. The plan dated 1592, derived from Hammond's map of Cambridge, shows Old Court as it would have appeared by about 1389; that dated 1682 is based on Loggan's view (figure 39).

In planning the new building there was a natural desire on the part of the College to keep the well-built Master's Lodge if possible and various schemes were devised which attempted to do this. The most fully developed of these was in the form of a simple building with rooms on four floors. However, from the outset it was clear that this would be an uncomfortable neighbour to the Lodge and the use made of the site would be poor.

After rejection of this scheme by the College in 1992, the brief was redefined and it was accepted that the existing Lodge would have to be demolished. The freedom this gave allowed a swift development of the key characteristics of the scheme as it now stands. The brief drawn up by the Buildings Committee and honed by the constraints of the site provided for a complex and socially rich mix of parts, which allowed architectural interest and differentiation to occur as a natural reflection of the content and context of the building.

In outline the development has 92 student rooms, a Fellow's set, a large seminar room, a student common room and a new Master's Lodge. In the basement are music practice rooms, a computer room, an exercise room, a laundry and storage. Some car parking is also provided. The College's brief added four stipulations, all of which we have tried to meet: that the building should be of its time; have a long life expectancy and not use untested technologies; should be good value for money; and be the best twentieth-century collegiate development in Cambridge.

The design largely emerged from consideration of two factors: the relationship of the parts of the building to the city and the College, and the design of a typical student room, which in turn helped to determine the elevations.

The new building offers a clear and simple geometry to the College, the two wings meeting at a right angle, with the junction marked by a lantern over the principal stair. Each end of the L-shaped configuration terminates positively; at the west with the new Master's Lodge, which acts as a buffer between the Peterhouse Lodge and the rest of the building, and to the north with an expansion in the depth of the building which allows the introduction of a cloistered raised garden above the ground-level parking. The bulk of the building is drawn back from the street, rather than hugging the perimeter of the College, and three projections from it create a series of small spaces between them which have been developed as a sequence of peripheral court gardens. The largest of the projections is surmounted by the lantern already mentioned, and provides a new entrance into the College from Tennis Court Road.

The standard student room is modest but not cramped and has a generous floor-to-ceiling height. The relatively deep plan allows a greater density of rooms per length of building than elsewhere in the College and this is increased by the use of corridors, punctuated at

Figure 105 The new building nearing completion in October 1997. The range to the left is the Nihon University Wing, so named to commemorate a major benefaction from that university towards the cost of the building.

Figure 106 (opposite) The Orchard in early Spring, Ivy Court in the background. The gardens are one of the delights of Pembroke. Garden and buildings form a whole; in moving through the College one necessarily walks through the garden and, because no court is fully enclosed, one constantly catches glimpses of other parts of the garden. Figure 104 shows that despite the nineteenth- and twentieth-century developments, the garden still occupies most of the site.

intervals by stairs and gyp rooms. Each room is planned to allow a number of different configurations of bed, desk and other furniture; each has a recessed storage and washing area the length of one half of the room depth, mirrored with that of the adjacent room. This interlocking design creates the order of the principal elevations, with thicker and thinner wall divisions between rooms alternating and manifest as trabeated piers of stone. Each room has two windows; the smaller more discreet, lighting one wall, the larger the full height of the room but in two parts, the upper of clear glass, the lower translucent. The windows are placed deeply in the facade and a bay is formed by the long stone lintel which is the width of the room. The choice of stone was critical and the budget, quarried sizes, tone and durability all played a part in the decision. After visits to twenty-three limestone quarries and mines and inspections of buildings in France and England, Bath base bed was chosen, with a harder French stone for the plinth of the building.

Successful examples of stone used in contemporary architecture are the exception rather than the rule. Nonetheless, stone has played an important part in the tradition of modernism in buildings in which the rhetoric of industrialization and technology was tempered by a sense of cultural continuity; an innovative fusion is found notably in the work of the Comasco architects of the early 1930s and there are other examples from the 1960s, particularly in Cambridge. The stone construction technique used on the new building is neither load-bearing masonry nor cladding but a self-supporting skin, making use of possibilities offered by modern quarrying and laying techniques.

The building was always intended to act as a backdrop to new College gardens, and not as a celebration of its own presence. The earliest sketch proposals suggested a series of distinct buildings – an informality based on the precedent of the Beiguinage of the Low Countries. An echo of this idea is to be seen in the completed building in both the roof and in the stair locations, which in their relative transparency create breaks between groups of rooms. West of the principal court are the interwoven spaces of the Master's and Fellows' Gardens, diminished compared with their previous sizes but echoing the adjacencies of Loggan's seventeenth-century view of the College (figure 39). The peripheral courtyard gardens add greatly to the spirit of quietitude to be expected in a building of this kind and help to mediate between the streets of the city and the College interior.

In choosing in 1987 a relatively young and little-known architectural practice the College was, I think, seeking a designer with whom to develop a scheme rather than one who might impose a solution. Contemporary architecture is not generally highly regarded by Cambridge dons. However, from the architects' position the built

environment is ultimately a reflection of a collective will and good buildings are made as much by the client as the designer. There has certainly been constructive dialogue and as the building nears completion we can look back on over sixty formal meetings at which we have presented and discussed ideas. I have been reminded from time to time that we have to a large extent been given a free rein and allowed to do much as we considered appropriate, if under an always alert and watchful eye.

Eric Parry

The War Memorials, 1914–18 and 1939–45

Adjacent to the Chapel, on the cloister piers, are the names of 149 undergraduates and one College servant killed on active service during the 1939–45 war. The names are inscribed on bronze plaques designed by Murray Easton. They are listed by year of matriculation and include the man's name and initials as well as regiment or service arm. The memorial was unveiled by the Master and dedicated by the Bishop of Ely, Edward Wynn (formerly Tutor) at a service held on 10 July 1948.

Facing these plaques are the names carved in stone of 305 Pembroke men and three College servants who died in the 1914–18 war. This memorial was designed by T. H. Lyons, and was unveiled and dedicated on 3 December 1924. These names are also listed by year of matriculation, and include service details.

There are several distinctive features of the Pembroke war memorials. The first is their egalitarian character. There is no distinction of rank; all who fell are equal. The second is the prominence given to the Great War losses, visible from First Court, and the more hidden, intimate nature of the names of those who died in the 1939–45 war.

The first of these elements – egalitarianism – is a feature common to many, though not all, Cambridge college war memorials. Peterhouse lists its 'lost generation' by rank. The second element – the prominence of 1914–18 losses – is not the general pattern in Cambridge colleges. Visitors to Trinity College chapel, for example, will be struck first by the names of those who died in the 1939–45 war, listed prominently in the ante-chapel, before proceeding to the 1914–18 war memorial in the chapel itself.

The Pembroke format is economical of space and cost, but it reflects wider currents of thought as well. The commemorative movement after the 1914–18 war was conducted in the spirit that such a catastrophe could never happen again. The inscription in Latin – 'The memory of the 300 sons of this house who gave their life as soldiers for their country is alive' – is both elegiac and hortatory. But the warning did not hold, and the loss of life recurred. After 1945, the

Figure 107 The Hitcham Cloister, with the War Memorials: 1914–18 left, 1939–45 right.

Latin inscription echoes the first: 'these gave their life for love of the same country and with the same virtue'. The inscription urges us to see these two lists as casualties of the same earthquake, with tremors 25 years apart. This is hardly surprising, since the grammar of commemoration of the 1914–18 war dominated remembrance of the Second World War. In the Cambridge town war memorial on Station Road, the names of those who died in the 1939–45 conflict are added to those who fell 25 years before. This is true throughout Britain. It was perhaps inevitable, therefore, that the names of Pembroke men who died in the Second World War should fall, as it were, in the shadow of those who died in the First.

What of the men whose names are inscribed there? A few brief remarks may help identify to us, decades later, what was vivid to generations of undergraduates who passed that way in the course of the academic year. The first is the sheer scale of loss in the 1914–18 war. The 305 Pembroke men who died form 27 per cent of all Pembroke men who served. This is roughly twice the national average, and well above the average for the University as a whole – 18 per cent killed of those who served. The terrifyingly high casualties increase as the year of matriculation approaches 1914. Fully 30 per cent of those who matriculated in the course of the last year of peace were killed in the conflict. These staggering statistics of loss are explained by the fact that almost all Pembroke men who served were officers, and officers' casualty rates were twice those of men in the ranks. (One of those who died was Captain Eric Dougall (matriculated 1904) who was posthumously awarded the Victoria Cross for bravery and leadership in action near Messines on 10 April 1918.) Of the 1140 Pembroke men who served, only 18 were private soldiers. Of the 24 College servants in uniform, three were killed. This is in line with national casualty rates of one in eight killed.

The Second World War casualties reflect another facet of the College's contribution to the war effort. Of the 149 men who died, 51 had served in the Royal Air Force. The infantryman's war of 1914–18 was lethal for junior officers; the air war, 25 years later, for flying officers. One of those who died was Jock Butler, younger son of the Master, Sir Montagu Butler.

Given the scale and dispersed nature of the two wars, these lists are necessarily incomplete. Some names were added after the memorials were dedicated; others have never been so honoured. A full list may be found in the College Library, where there is an annotated copy of the College's war record.

Another element of incompleteness reflects the military character of commemoration. Here again the First World War model lingered. The Second World War was a civilians' war too, but Pembroke men who died as a result of enemy action are not included.

Pembroke's commemorative history of the two world wars begins in the cloister but does not end there. Loss of life in war was marked in other ways, reflecting the unity of Pembroke's civilian and military victims. One example must suffice to illustrate this point. E. A. Nahum came up as a scholar from Clifton in 1936. He worked at the Cavendish Laboratory on deuteron bombardment of the heavy elements. He was killed in an air raid on Cambridge, and his parents established a memorial fund in his name. Others were commemorated through the War Memorial and Sexcentenary Fund created in 1945.

J. M. Winter

'Monty' and 'Rab'

Since the eighteenth century, the Butler family has produced many distinguished academics, churchmen and public servants. In the last hundred years, one branch of it has enjoyed particularly close connections with Pembroke. Sir Montagu Butler was an undergraduate and, after a distinguished career in India, Master from 1937 to 1948; his son, R. A. Butler, graduated in 1925 and was then briefly a Fellow of Corpus before becoming an eminent politician. Both were elected Honorary Fellows of Pembroke, in 1924 and 1941. They are both striking examples of the marriage of two philosophies: of commitment to the public service and to the cause of academic excellence.

Montagu Butler came up to Pembroke from Haileybury in 1891. He was an outstanding classical scholar, who took firsts in both parts of the tripos, but he was also energetic in several other fields: he was President of the Cambridge Union, cox of the College boat, and founder of the College Ball. He was elected to a Fellowship in 1895 but came top in the examinations for the Indian Civil Service the next year and, like his elder brother, decided to devote his career to public service in the sub-continent.

The reputation of the Indian Civil Service was then at its height. It was able to recruit from among the country's academic elite. It needed men suited to the business of classifying vast amounts of data about the Indian population and able to find dextrous solutions to difficult administrative problems. India fired the imagination of young university graduates because it seemed to offer a route to eminence in the state, a satisfying mental challenge, and a socially worthwhile role, especially for those with pronounced humanitarian or religious views. Clive Dewey's book, *Anglo-Indian Attitudes* (1993), describes in detail the outlook of F. L. Brayne, an evangelical Pembroke undergraduate slightly younger than Monty, who devoted his life to the ICS.

Monty was sent to the Punjab. Conscientious, intense and clearheaded, he threw himself fully into the work of providing good government for the Indians. As Settlement Officer in Kotah State for five years, he would move from village to village with a train of camels, assessing the land, receiving petitions and dispensing judgment. In his autobiography, his son wrote of him: 'I have never known a human being with quite such an acute sense of responsibility; it made him morose and anxious, but it was used at all times for the good of the people of India as he saw their needs'.

Monty rose quickly through the Service; he became a Deputy Commissioner in 1909 and, after a number of desk jobs, was Governor of the Central Provinces between 1925 and 1933. He was an outstandingly gifted administrator, energetic, thorough, quick, yet

Figure 108 Sir Montagu Butler (1873–1952). Pencil drawing by Francis Dodd (1945), presented by his son, R.A. Butler.

endlessly patient in reconciling clashing views. In his own generation he was a liberal in dealing with the native population, and Rab was brought up to regard the Indians as friends. But he shared some of the postwar demoralisation in the ICS as the home government's actions began to undermine its authority and status and was not sorry when, with the help of Rab (then a junior minister at the India Office), he was brought back from India in 1933 to be Lieutenant-Governor of the Isle of Man. Four years later he was elected Master of Pembroke.

He was an outstanding Master for eleven years; his tenure was extended until the statutory limit. He brought to bear all his administrative gifts (especially necessary when Fellows departed for war service), his unwavering commitment to service, and his tact and tolerance in dealing with independently minded colleagues. As Meredith Dewey wrote, 'he was habituated to oriental habits of pro-

Figure 109 Lord Butler. Portrait by Allan Gwynne-Jones (1964). Painted when R.A. Butler was Foreign Secretary.

crastination, and realized that an indefatigable pertinacity was the only procedure to budge academics'. This strategy was remarkably successful. He also wanted to see Pembroke men play their part in the wider world. When the Tutor, Edward Wynn, was asked to be Bishop of Ely, Monty, who had no time for clerical or any other humbug, urged him to accept at once, despite the loss to the college: 'no nonsense about father praying in the study while mother is packing in the bedroom'. He was unashamedly devoted to the College. At the university luncheon in June 1947 to celebrate Pembroke's 600th anniversary, he spoke of the College colours, 'which we have worn and striven proudly for in our young days, and in later life never see again without something of a thrill'. Meredith Dewey recounts how he always came to College concerts and asked the provenance of the performers. 'If he was told they came from Clare or Corpus he would remove his hearing aid and without complaint or rancour close his eyes'. The Pembroke Butlers were not musical.

Both Monty's sons came to the College; the younger, Jock, was tragically killed in the Second World War. Monty gave the elder the initials R.A.B. in order to provide him with a sobriquet that would be useful in a public career. Though Rab took firsts in French and History and, like his father, could have remained a Cambridge don, there was no doubting his commitment to a political life. He wrote to Monty in 1923, 'I must do something active . . . Pembroke dons are sleek and affable and content themselves with saying that the modern world is dirty. It may be, but there is much to be done.' A President of the Union, with ambitions to be Viceroy of India, could not content himself with an academic post. He became Conservative MP for Saffron Walden in 1929 and from 1932 to 1964 was never off the front benches of the Commons. In the 1930s he was successively a junior minister for India, Labour and the Foreign Office; from 1941 to 1945 he was a path-breaking President of the Board of Education; and from 1951 to 1964 he was in turn Chancellor of the Exchequer, Leader of the House of Commons, Home Secretary, Deputy Prime Minister and Foreign Secretary.

Monty had advised Rab that he was not decisive enough to reach the top in politics and that his forte was subtlety and diplomacy. This was a characteristically forthright judgment. The successes and longevity of Rab's career partly disprove it, but he will always be remembered as the man who was passed over three times for the premiership by the Conservative party establishment (in 1955, 1957 and 1963). There were several reasons for these rejections, including his willingness, in the 1930s, to execute the policy of appeasing the dictators, his disdain, in the 1950s, for right-wing prejudices on social issues, and his unwillingness, at any time, to organise a campaign or otherwise cause trouble on his own behalf. Churchill is supposed to have thought that he lacked the vision of a true leader: he was too equivocal, too much the compromising administrator. Some Conservatives accused him of intellectual condescension; they found him aloof, unfathomable, astringent or whimsical in personal dealings. (His 'Rabisms' became famous. One was his remark, at a party, 'We are so glad to have got here in time to see you leave'; another was his comment, *á propos* Lord Home: 'I may never have known much about ferrets or flower-arranging but one thing I did know was how to govern the people of this country'.) Rab himself began his memoirs with the remark that he had spent his career perched on a 'tripos', with one leg in academia, one in politics, and one in his Indian administrative upbringing, and this was an acute remark. He was too much the detached and subtle academic, and too much the loyal state servant, to be a ruthless or populist politician. Iain Macleod observed that, 'Rab loves being a politician

Figure 110 Pennell's biscuit box. Designed by Sir Ellis Minns (Fellow, 1913–1953) and given in 1953 by Vernon Pennell (Fellow, 1914–1976).

among academics and an academic among politicians'; Baldwin, half-teasingly, accused him of the 'sin of intellectualism'.

But his academic and administrative talents account also for some of the greatest achievements of his political career. His 1944 Act was a major milestone in the extension of state education, and was achieved by patient negotiation with religious leaders every bit as difficult as the factions that his father had dealt with in India. As long-standing chairman of the Conservative Research Department, he created a college-like atmosphere of open debate, attracted able young men to work for the party, and so did an enormous amount to erode its ingrained prejudices, by introducing more thinking men into the Commons and by bombarding constituency associations with pamphlets and speakers. Like his father, Rab was a proconsular figure, committed to the notion that academic excellence should be directed to serving the state, and that by doing so civilised and humane values would be promoted. His thirteen-year reign as Master of Trinity College, from 1965 to 1978, was a fitting end to his career and possibly its happiest episode.

Jonathan Parry

Figure 111 Covered caudle cup. A modern copy of one at The Queen's College, Oxford, our sister College, given by them in 1932 to mark the alliance made then between Queen's and Pembroke. The original was given to Queen's by one of their greatest benefactors, Sir Joseph Williamson, who was educated at St Bees School, to which both Queen's and Pembroke appoint governors and which was founded by a common benefactor, Edmund Grindall.

Figure 112 Casket sent in 1947 by Pembroke College, Providence, Rhode Island, to contain an address of congratulation on our sexcentenary. This Pembroke College is the women's college of Brown University and bears Pembroke's name in honour of our Roger Williams, founder of Rhode Island. Designed by J. Russell Price; made by Gorham Co., Providence.

Figure 113 Edward Granville Browne (1862–1926).

Oriental Studies at Pembroke

A notable strand in Pembroke's academic history in recent decades has been its commitment to supporting this minority subject, so maintaining a stimulating diversity in the College's student and scholarly population.

The Tripos is itself a relatively recent addition to the Cambridge curricula: the first Board of Oriental Studies met in 1866. The Tripos in Semitic Languages followed in 1878, the Single Oriental Languages Tripos (including Arabic and Persian) started in 1895, Turkish being added in 1902, Chinese in 1913 and Japanese not until 1948. The present Faculty of Oriental Studies dates back only to 1968. Pembroke's Oriental connection goes back almost to the beginning of this development. E. G. Browne, undoubtedly our most renowned figure in this field, came up to Pembroke in 1879, where he began by reading medicine. By the time he became a Fellow in 1893, however, his commitment to Persian was assured (following a trip immortalised in his book, *A Year Amongst the Persians*), and he became Sir Thomas Adams's Professor of Arabic in 1902, a post he held until his death in 1926. Browne's legacy was enormous, not only in his published work, but in the books, manuscripts, newspapers, documents and photographs he left to the University and to College, which also has a Fund and a Prize established in his name.

Among the Pembroke students of Browne's time who later achieved academic distinction was Laurence Lockhart (d. 1959), who took a first in Arabic and Persian in 1915 and later published *Nadir Shah* (1938) and *The Fall of the Safavi Dynasty* (1958), which have remained standard works on eighteenth-century Persian history.

Pembroke's second Professor of Arabic was A. J. Arberry, who came to the College in 1924 and took a double first in Classics and Oriental Languages (1929). He returned to Cambridge and Pembroke in 1947 and remained a Fellow until his death in 1969. Arberry was a prolific writer, producing more than fifty books, mostly bringing the major works of Arabic and Persian literature to a wider audience through translations and editions. *The Koran Interpreted* (1955) is perhaps the most significant of these. It was Arberry who set up the Cambridge Centre of Middle Eastern Studies, which started life in 1960 in a small office hired from the College.

During Arberry's time, Pembroke offered a berth to Erwin Rosenthal (d. 1991), lecturer in Hebrew and a distinguished scholar of Arabic and Islamic philosophy, who came to Cambridge in 1948 and was made a Fellow in 1962. His most important published work is probably his *Political Thought in Medieval Islam* (1958).

More recently, Malcolm Lyons, who retired in 1996 after fifty years of association with College and eleven as Professor of Arabic, became

Figure 114 Sir William Hodge (1903–75). Lowndean Professor of Astronomy and Geometry; FRS; elected Fellow, 1935; Master, 1958–70.

Sir William Hodge, whose subject was algebraic geometry, was the founder of a notable Pembroke mathematical tradition. His pupil, Sir Michael Atiyah (Fellow, 1958–61; Savilian Professor of Geometry at Oxford, FRS, Master of Trinity College; Honorary Fellow, 1983), ranged widely over pure mathematics, especially geometry and topology. He taught as undergraduates Sir John Kingman (Research Fellow, 1961–65; professorship at Oxford, 1969; FRS; Vice-Chancellor of the University of Bristol; Honorary Fellow, 1989), who specialised in probability theory and statistics, and W. B. R. Lickorish, topologist (Fellow from 1964). The latter in turn taught topology and geometry to Simon Donaldson (Wallis Professor of Mathematics at Oxford, 1985; FRS; Honorary Fellow, 1992). Distinguished Pembroke mathematicians standing outside this lineage include Robert Stoneley, theoretical geophysicist (Fellow 1943–1976; FRS) and Brandon Carter, cosmologist (Research Fellow 1967–71; FRS).

(For further details of Pembroke mathematicians see the article by J. P. Dougherty in *PCCS Annual Gazette*, **60** (1986).

Figure 115 William Anthony Camps (Fellow, 1933–97; Tutor, 1947–62; Master, 1970–81.) A classical scholar, distinguished for his editions of Propertius and for his books on Homer and Virgil's *Aeneid*, Tony Camps was probably the most influential Fellow this century in shaping the modern College.

the third Pembroke incumbent of the Chair this century. His latest, but not his last, contribution to the field is his three-volume study of *The Arabian Epic* (1995). During this long period, a strong Scottish connection was introduced into Arabic studies, with former Pembroke graduate students and Research Fellows filling University posts in Glasgow and St Andrews. Malcolm Lyons established the Pembroke Arabic Research Group, using funds generated by the sale of his own editions of Arabic scientific texts, and in a similar vein the College is now associated with a series entitled *Pembroke Papers*, devoted to publishing research on Persian history and culture.

Current generations of Pembroke undergraduates are fortunate in enjoying the results of the College's long and distinguished association with Oriental Studies, and particularly the Middle East, access to which is invaluably supported by two travel funds, one established in memory of Derek Rose, killed in the Yemen, and another recently inaugurated in the names of Erwin and Elizabeth Rosenthal.

Charles Melville

Figure 116 The Master's Chair. Black bean veneer over bent beech plywood, the coat of arms in Bombay rosewood and with morocco upholstery. Designed and carved by David Pye and made and upholstered by R. Lenthall at the Royal College of Art. Presented in 1954 by F. C. and J. C. Pritchard (Pembroke, 1920; died 1992) in memory of their father and of F. C. Pritchard's son. The chair is important as the first example of the mid twentieth-century style in official Cambridge furnishings.

Music in Pembroke

Although music was taught in the medieval University as part of the *quadrivium* of the standard degree course, what was taught bore little relation to the performance of music. There is no surviving evidence of the former in Pembroke and little of the latter. Early statutes exhort the Dean to encourage the learning of plainsong, for the better ordering of Chapel services. Annotations by Matthew Wren from sources now lost provide other glimpses. They record a payment for an organ player in 1470, one for musicians at a feast in 1531, a receipt of 33s 4d for 'organs' (an organ in our terminology) sold in 1567, and a fee of 50s paid for a music lecture, or perhaps lectureship, in 1585. The lecturer was presumably Thomas Mudd, who took his MA in 1584 and became a Fellow soon afterwards. Many compositions by Mudd survive, of which the best known is probably the anthem *Let thy merciful ears O Lord*, but since his father, brother and nephew were also active composers, it is not always clear which member of the family wrote what. He left Cambridge in 1592. A near-contemporary is Thomas Ravenscroft, composer of consort and church music, particularly remembered for his collection of sturdy hymn tunes in *The Whole Booke of Psalmes* (1621).

There are two important seventeenth-century artefacts. The first is the set of so-called Pembroke choir-books: six manuscript volumes, one per voice, in a collection that originally must have had eight and an organ volume. They date from 1625 to *c.* 1640, and new items, in various hands, were added as needs grew. The collection contains no music not known from other sources except for a Kyrie and Creed by Farrant (of whom there were four, with problems of ascription as with the Mudds). The current belief is that the volumes were in use elsewhere before being given to the College by Henry May (admitted 1637, Fellow 1642). They were probably used in the Wren Chapel in its early years (there is one post-Restoration anthem), but then lay forgotten in the College library until rediscovery in the 1950s.

The second artefact is the organ currently in Framlingham church, Suffolk, a College living, to which it was given in 1708, having originally been in the College Chapel. The general belief now is that this was built for the Wren Chapel by Thomas Thamar in 1674. Rather more of the Thamar organ survives at Framlingham than does of its 1708 Quarles/Smith successor at Pembroke, though both have undergone Victorianisation and de-Victorianisation. The Framlingham organ contains most of its original Great chorus, including in particular the cornet-mixture rescued in 1970 from an attic in the former Rectory, so that one can still appreciate its rich seventeenth-century sound. The Pembroke organist of the time, also organist at King's College, was Thomas Tudway (*c.* 1650–1726), a composer but remembered mainly for his compilations of cathedral music.

In 1708 the College replaced the Thamar organ with the one by

Figure 117 Sir Arthur Bliss. Drawing by Richard Stone (1983).

Charles Quarles, which is substantially the one that stands today. Quarles was perhaps more an organ-assembler than a builder, in that he sometimes bought sets of pipes 'off the shelf' as required. The surviving wooden pipes, which form the acoustic core of the present instrument, were made by 'Father' Bernard Smith, and contribute much to its conspicuous sense of high-quality; they may also contribute to its sense of loudness in that, being designed for nowhere in particular, they are probably larger than Smith would have used for our small and resonant Chapel.

The only known Pembroke organist of the eighteenth century was Peter Hellendaal (1721–1799). Born in Rotterdam, he came to England in 1751 and Pembroke in 1762. He deserted Pembroke for Peterhouse in 1777. The other eighteenth-century Pembroke figure of musical importance was Edward Hussey Delaval, Fellow in 1751, a chemist (FRS 1759) and a collaborator of Benjamin Franklin via their interest in lightning. His musical fame was as a performer on musical glasses, which when rubbed give a sweet but disembodied tone ('a Cherubim in a box': Thomas Gray). Franklin, fascinated by the sound, mechanised the action of the glasses to produce a practicable musical instrument, the *armonica*, in which form it became known to Mozart whose exquisite quintet K617 it provoked in 1791.

The College underwent rapid and radical expansion in the 1870s. Music was represented by work on the organ, by William Hill in 1863 and Thomas Hill in 1872, followed by a grand enlargement by Norman & Beard in 1902. The College's most distinguished music student, and its first for many years, arrived a few years later: Arthur Bliss (1891–1975), who took his BA and Mus.B in 1913. His compositions, of which the most famous are probably the *Colour Symphony* (1922), the ballet *Checkmate* and the clarinet quintet, combine the atonality of their times with Edwardian grandeur via Elgar, a close personal friend. He was knighted in 1950 and became Master of the Queen's Musick in 1953.

The next Pembroke Mus.B was Patrick ('Paddy') Hadley (1899–1973), son of W. S. Hadley, Fellow from 1882 and Master 1912–1927. Both composer and teacher, he was Professor of Music and Fellow of Caius 1946–1962; his best known work is the short anthem *My beloved spake*. A successor as both Pembroke Mus.B and Professor of Music was Robert ('Robin') Orr, organ scholar 1929–32, distinguished composer and currently Honorary Fellow.

With Orr's period as undergraduate, Pembroke music begins to assume its modern form. Chapel music was in the charge of an undergraduate organ scholar, with a volunteer amateur choir and no professional senior musical direction, a pattern that has continued to the present day. The choir incorporated town boys, with a Chaplain-run scout-cub pack, until the War, when in the absence of

Figure 118 Matriculation photograph in preparation, 1988.

the Dean the organ scholar brought in women, Pembroke being the first Cambridge chapel choir to do so. Recreative music was represented by a Music, or Musical, Society, which, so far as *Gazette* records (1927 onwards) go, first appeared with a brief entry describing 'a concert' under Orr's Presidency, of Elizabethan and other songs and recorder music on 24 May 1931.

From about the middle of the twentieth century, music as a fact of everyday life became transformed out of recognition by the ready availability of broadcast and recorded performances. Serious music was no longer the specialist interest of a determined few, and present undergraduates probably know more Beethoven than Shakespeare; many of them have performed in his symphonies at school. The changes in activity of the Music Society in the last fifty years reflect this changing and growing awareness. The Pembroke Singers, or the Choral Society as it was earlier known, was the main focus of activity from about 1950 to 1965, with the Valence-Mary Singers an elite offshoot specialising in madrigals; a baroque orchestra, the 'Pembaroque' succeeded them from 1965 to about 1972. Since then there has been no clear pattern other than that of steady growth, in range and scale and expertise. A measure of the change since 1931 is that on 6 March 1993 the Music Society performed Bach's *St Matthew Passion*, in German, with proper orchestration, and in its entirety, with forces, soloists and some obbligatists apart, drawn mostly from within the College.

One of the most ebullient conductors of the Pembroke Singers was David Munrow (1942–1976), who came up in 1961. With his contemporary Christopher Hogwood (Pembroke 1960, now Honorary Fellow) he formed the Early Music Consort of London in 1967, and began a short but explosive career. With a deep insight into what had stimulated medieval and Renaissance composers to write as they had, an uncanny virtuosity on every wind instrument he touched, and a brilliantly entertaining style of public presentation, he blazoned the cause of early music played on instruments of its day to a spell-bound world. He is one of the great influential musicians of his generation.

Two important events punctuate the last fifty years. One was the admission of women to the College in 1983, which *inter alia* allowed recruitment of mixed choirs from within the College's own membership. The other was the rebuilding of the organ in 1980 by Mander, which uncompromisingly restored it to the style and size of the 1708 original. As rebuilt it is excellent for the early repertory, including Bach, and inevitably not easy for later music, particularly for accompanying anthems in the nineteenth- and twentieth-century cathedral tradition. But the many thrilling performances since 1980 of music by Franck, Liszt, Widor, etc make nonsense of the dismissive view, occasionally aired, that the organ is 'quite unsuitable' for music of the romantic period.

The scale of music-making in present-day Cambridge is breathtaking. A few years ago a keen instrumentalist, reading mathematics, brightly remarked to his tutor at the end of his first term that since coming up in October he had played in forty-nine concerts. One may marvel at his energy, but qua opportunity it would not have been at all difficult. Inevitably the quality of such music-making is variable, as is the degree of preparation. But the combination of quality and quantity is remarkable, and in a world where the amateur/professional divide has yet to harden, there are many memorable performances. As with other areas besides music, the intensity and the scale of Cambridge activity provides a proving ground for those for whom, as with David Munrow, what was a hobby as an undergraduate becomes a life's work thereafter.

Sidney Kenderdine

For further information see the following articles in *PCCS Annual Gazette*: 'The organ in Framlingham church', **45** (1971); 'Mr Delaval's Glasses', **57** (1983); 'The Organ' (rebuilding by Mander), **55** (1981); 'David John Munrow', **50** (1976).

Sport

As that sixteenth-century all-rounder Nicholas Ridley attests,[1] from early on there were archery, bowls and tennis. Horse-play with a football was briefly tolerated at the Restoration, but other ancestors of today's games were forbidden as common and riotous. The tennis court abutted the orchard and remained there, along the road which now bears its name, until New Court was built on the site in 1881. Otherwise undergraduates took their exercise in field sports if they had means, or in fetching and carrying if sizars. Then began the modern public schools, cradles of practically every European popular sport. Rules were drawn up for games at school, early fixtures arranged against other schools, the moving spirits removed to university, shortly afterwards the first inter-collegiate matches were held and then, with a lag of hardly a year or two, either the first Oxford and Cambridge match, or the first international. Rowing and cricket, *sui generis* to be sure, inaugurated the series of contests in the 1830s, rackets followed in the mid 1850s, athletics in the early 1860s, the two footballs and golf in the 1870s – with more specialist pursuits, from polo to cycling, scattered among them. Hockey and boxing came last, in 1890 and 1897. Fenners' ground dates from 1852. A visit by Baron de Coubertin in 1887 is thought to have planted in the Baron's mind the idea of the modern Olympics.

1 See Willis and Clark, *Architectural history of the University of Cambridge*, vol. III, p. 577.

Pembroke joined the movement with some delay, quickly made up. In 1858 there had been only one freshman (p. 109) and in 1869 the College was still smallest in numbers after King's and Downing. By 1919, however, it was largest but for Trinity and Caius (and larger in undergraduate numbers than it is today). With this came games. The first 'blue' was a Harrovian from Kendal with the apt and familiar name of Aymer Ainslie, a Pembroke grandson as well as great-grandfather, who dominated university rackets from 1860 to 1863 and founded an engineering firm. The next two were northerners also: Joseph Bowstead Wilson from Giggleswick, who rowed at '4' in the 1863 boat, and Howard Watson, a Cumbrian from Manchester Grammar, '3' in the 1864 boat. Like so many other blues, both were later ordained. But the fourth was a Londoner educated privately, Walter Norman Powys. He secured his first blue in 1871, played for the Gentlemen in 1872, and then for Hampshire. Bearded and apt to impersonate the Prince of Wales, Powys was a famously fast left-hand bowler who in the 1871 university match took 6 for 49, and on the second day of the 1874 match, in 3 overs and 3 balls, disposed of the remaining 4 wickets without a run from the bat being scored off his bowling. All the same, on both occasions Oxford won. Against another dark blue XI with no fewer than eight Gentlemen he took 13 for 78. Powys did not graduate until 1879, then read at the Bar, went to America, and like a number of other distinguished Pembroke sportsmen died relatively young, accidentally.

Blues may not tell the entire story of Pembroke's ascendancy, yet speak eloquently. Over the 1870s in each of the major sports two Pembroke men achieved the distinction of a blue, often repeatedly. In athletics there were three, including in 1874 the AAA champion in the 100 yards and long jump (the Cliftonian E. J. Davies). The blues in Rugby football each played for England. (By 1900–1913, however, there was to be an annual average of three Rugby blues, including the mighty William Cobby, selected for England ahead of his blue, and C. N. Lowe, an Alleynian winger who scored 18 tries for England on either side of the Great War.) The 1880s saw the first antipodean colonials among Pembroke blues, the first Scottish international – the Fettesian C. J. B. Milne, killed in a railway accident aged 30 – as well the first blue in more than one sport (T. H. Marsh, a high jumper and footballer from New Zealand). Then begins the succession of familiar names echoing down the generations: Block, Stobart, Streatfeild, McGougan, van der Byl, Preston, Lowe, MacMyn, and on. In 1886 the College boat won the Ladies' Plate at Henley.

By the 1890s, although there were still only two blues at Rugby – both of them however blues repeatedly and both from Cheltenham College – in Association football there were twelve (among them S.S. Taylor, an early director of Anglo-American); six in cricket and in golf; and five in athletics, including the AAA half-mile champion

(H.W. Workman from Repton, who dominated the Harvard and Yale matches of 1899). In 1891 R. Thompson, an Irish forward, went on the first, Rhodes-funded, British ('Lions') tour of South Africa. In 1895 Pembroke supplied five of the University's footballers, yet the light blues lost. Blues at more than one sport or among denizens of the same Pembroke tribe were becoming more commonplace. E. C. Streatfeild, W. W. Lowe, and L. J. Moon belong to those with blues at both cricket and Association football. (In 1907 the Rossallian F. H. Mugliston beat them by adding golf to the other two.) Streatfeild, not the last of that name to be a blue – the 'C' stands for Champion – a Carthusian who played for Surrey, made 30 and took 4 wickets (one being C. B. Fry's) for 19 runs in the second innings of the 1893 match; he had won the public schools' rackets competition for good measure. Lowe, from Malvern, played for Worcestershire and became a noted skater, author also of the *Bedrock Principles of Golf*. His contemporary W. G. Grace, son of the doctor, played Rugby for Northamptonshire, as well as cricket of course for Gloucestershire, and died aged 31; he was an all-rounder, unfortunately out for ducks in both innings of the 1896 university match. Moon, the first Pembroke cricketer to go on to play for England (in 1906), opened the Cambridge batting and in 1900 scored 113 in the first innings at Lords. He was killed with the Devons at Salonika in 1916. His golfing contemporary, the Wykehamist E. F. Wood, survived to be deported from Guernsey to Germany during the Second War. Another Wood (G. E. C.) was the last pre-war blue, and the first to return to the crease – from the Gloucesters with an MC – in the university match at Lords in 1919, as well as in the pack at Twickenham in the same year.

In the 1920s Pembroke sport reached a high-water mark. In 1921 the hockey was won and the final of the Colquhouns was an in-house affair – K. N. Craig beating T. D. A. Collet. The latter was to break several records in 1926, in a private match rowed over the Boat Race course, narrowly beating the Olympic champion Jack Beresford in 21 minutes 32 seconds. The College boat house had been built in 1896 and for forty-three years it was run with equanimity by Fred Foister as boatman ('Well, sir, you must experiment, you won't get anywhere without experiments'). In 1923 Pembroke went head of the river in the Mays and reached the final of the Grand Challenge at Henley. Collet rowed at '6'. (Further rowing successes were to follow in the 1930s, when for instance a blue boat dominated by Pembroke was to turn itself into the Olympic eight.) Ashore, H. G. Comber had become a Fellow in 1902. He was a Marlburian who captained the university at hockey in 1893, and as a Fellow proceeded to recruit a towering number of sportsmen. In this heyday Marlborough supplied most of the hockey players, Malvern and Harrow the cricketers, Charterhouse and

Figure 119 T. C. Livingstone-Learmonth (1924) winning the semi-final of the 400 metre hurdles, Amsterdam Olympics, July 1928.

2 A correspondent writes, 'In those days you did not marry till you had a place to live in. Cousins was for many years engaged to a lady from Coton by name of Neave, and the plan was for them to marry when the College provided a groundsman's house. This did not happen until 1938. I was at their wedding in Coton that year.' (J. C.)

Aldenham the soccer players, and Scotland the Rugby players. By the early 1920s Comber had cobbled together at Grantchester Meadows, from scattered parcels of land, the present sports ground. The present Pavilion was completed in 1939. With H.O. Cousins[2] as groundsman the Pembroke cricket pitch was used by the university as a preferred alternative to Fenners in the period between the wars.

Annus 1928 *mirabilis fuit*, the sixty-fifth year of modern Pembroke sport, where we stop (so as not to name the living, save one). The captains on tour of both the English Rugby and cricket teams were Pembroke. The former, W. W. Wakefield, later a politician, is thought by many to be England's greatest-ever Rugby player. The latter, A. P. F. Chapman, had been a Rugby blue too, and in 1926 was at 24 the youngest ever to captain the England XI – although, as far as the 1920s go, he was but the third from Pembroke to captain England at cricket. The other two, F. T. Mann and A. E. R. Gilligan, had both been victorious in series against the South Africans in 1922 and 1924. The captain of the Davis Cup team of 1928, H.W. ('Bunny') Austin, was Pembroke too; as was the English amateur golf champion, the Carthusian T. A.

Bourn. E. Martin Smith, who in 1928 had just come up, was to follow Bourn as open champion in 1931, the year that the Harrovian L. G. Crawley (1921) won the closed amateur contest for the first time. In the AAA championship of 1928, D. G. A. Lowe – 'young god on hot bricks' and gold medallist in the Paris Olympics of 1924 (800 metres) – won the quarter and half miles; while in the 440 yard hurdles, in which Lord Burghley set the world record at 54 seconds, T. C. Livingstone-Learmonth was second to Burghley. Livingstone-Learmonth was not 26 when, three years after the Amsterdam Olympics, he died of meningitis at Khartoum. There were sixteen blues in 1928, including the captains of both footballs and the President of CUBC, J. C. Holcroft, whose boat beat Oxford by 10 lengths 'in a paddle' in the Boat Race. D. H. E. McCowen inaugurated a run of PCBC victories in the Bushe – Foxe sculls. In the England–Scotland match at Twickenham the two English wing three-quarters, J. S. R. Reeve and C. C. Tanner, were Pembroke (neither of them yet a blue), and so in the Scottish pack was F. H. Waters, son of another Lorettonian Pembroke blue. On the Monday of a busy week at the end of the Lent term, 27 February to 3 March 1928, the inter-collegiate athletics was won outright for the fourth year in a six-year series; on the Wednesday the Rugby trophy was carried off in a ding-dong 13–11 final against Caius; and on Friday the other football knock-out, 2–0, again against Caius.

This survey stops short of the 1930s and, alas, even within the period under review much and many have not yet been mentioned. To name but a few at random in injury time: W. L. Raynes the cyclist who became mayor of Cambridge; M. Ll. Taylor the hockey player and war poet; E. S. Dougall, a long-distance runner from Tonbridge who was one of two VCs; A. R. Haigh-Brown the footballing author of *Sporting Sonnets*; and H. Ruttledge and L. R. Wager who, twenty years apart at Pembroke, were on the same early assault on Everest. Later there were to be J. H. T. Wilson, Olympic gold medallist at 37, and P. B. H. May, perhaps England's greatest post-War batsman, who opened his Test career with 138 at Leeds, but that is another story.

Michael Kuczynski

APPENDICES

Appendix A: Chronology

c. 1304	Birth of the Foundress, Marie de St Pol
1321	Marriage of the Foundress to Aymer de Valence, Earl of Pembroke
1324	Death of Aymer de Valence
1347	Edward III grants licence for foundation of the College
1355	Pope Innocent VI grants permission for building of a chapel
1377	Death of the Foundress
c. 1389	Old Court completed
1440	Benefactions of Henry VI
1450	Laurence Booth elected Master
1452	Library built above Hall
1480	Thomas Rotherham elected Master
c. 1483	William Lyndwood's *Provinciale* printed
1540	Nicholas Ridley elected Master
1551–68	Publication of William Turner's *Herbal*
1555	Martyrdom of Ridley
1559	Edmund Grindall elected Master
1564	Elizabeth I characterizes Pembroke as *'Domus antiqua et religiosa'*
1569	Edmund Spenser comes into residence
1589	Lancelot Andrewes elected Master
1636	Roger Williams founds settlement at Providence, Rhode Island
1614–70	North range of Ivy Court built
1636	Sir Robert Hitcham's bequest
1642	Matthew Wren, Bishop of Ely, imprisoned in Tower of London
1643	Dowsing purges chapel of 'superstitious imagery'
1646	Richard Crashaw's *Steps to the temple* published
1661	South range of Ivy Court completed (Peter Mills)
1665	New Chapel, gift of Matthew Wren, completed (Christopher Wren)
1682	Nehemiah Grew's *The anatomy of plants* published
1690	Old Chapel converted to library

1739	Christopher Smart comes into residence
1756	Thomas Gray migrates from Peterhouse to Pembroke
1773	William Pitt comes into residence
1807	Sara Lonsdale's bequest
1850	Stokes' formula for viscous drag published
1858	The one freshman admitted (Edward London Pincott) migrates to Gonville & Caius
1869	Change of Statutes allows Fellows to be married
1870	Death of Gilbert Ainslie; election of John Power as Master inaugurates College redevelopment
1872	Red Buildings (Waterhouse)
1873	Master's Lodge (Waterhouse)
1874–76	South range of Old Court, old Master's Lodge and old Hall demolished; new Hall (Waterhouse)
1878	New library (Waterhouse)
1881	Consecration of extension of Chapel (Scott)
1881	New Court built (Scott)
1885	College Mission founded
1894	Mallarmé lectures in Pembroke
1907	Pitt Building (Caröe)
1926	New rooms inserted above Hall
1928	W. W. Wakefield captains England at rugby
1929	Harry Guggenheim's first benefaction to Pembroke
1931	Gandhi visits Pembroke
1933	New Master's Lodge built (Webb)
1936	Aubrey Attwater's *Pembroke College, Cambridge: a short history* published
1957	Queen Elizabeth, The Queen Mother, visits Pembroke, the college of her forbears
1957	Orchard Building (Sisson)
1955	P. B. H. May captains England at cricket
1963	R. M. Dolby's first patent
1983	Valerie Kyle, first woman Fellow, elected; women graduate students admitted
1984	Admission of women undergraduates
1997	New building completed (Parry)

Appendix B: Masters of Pembroke College

In this list, dates in **bold** are verified from College registers, where these were kept up either contemporaneously with events, or nearly so, or from other sources considered to be reliable. Dates not in bold are considered to be the best available in the state of our knowledge. Where no satisfactory date exists, no date, or only a partial date is given. Where dates of both election and admission are known, these have been recorded, but presumably tenure of office dates from admission. Dates of death of those Masters who became bishops have been verified from the Royal Historical Society's *Handbook of British Chronology*, edited by Sir F. Maurice Powicke and E. B. Fryde (2nd ed. London 1961). For the medieval period, much use has been made of A. B. Emden, *Biographical Register of the University of Cambridge* (Cambridge, 1963), and also Venn's *Alumni Cantabrigienses*. All early names have a multiplicity of spellings.

Robert de Thorpe Master in 1354; until 1363 or 1364
Thomas de Bingham From 1364; died c. 1405
John Tynmouth or Tinmew Probably late 14th c.; died by 1389
Richard Morys c. 1385; still Master in 1392; died after 1404
John Sudbury 1406–1428; died c. 1435
John Langton 1428 until death; died 22 May 1447
Hugh Damlet 1447 until 1450; died 1476
Laurence Booth 1450; died 19 May 1480
Thomas Rotherham 1480–1488; died 29 May 1500
George Fitzhugh 1488; died 20 November 1505
Roger Leyburn 29 November 1505–1507; died 1507 or 1508: most published sources prefer 1508
Richard Foxe 7 August 1507–1518; died 5 October 1528
Robert Shorton 1518–34; died 17 October 1535
Robert Swinburn 1534–1537; died 10 February 1540
George Folberry 1537; died c. October 1540
Nicholas Ridley October 1540–53; burnt 16 October 1555
John Young 1554; deprived 20 July 1559; died 1579
Edmund Grindall 1559–1562; died 6 July 1583
Matthew Hutton 14 May 1562; resigned 1567; died 1605
John Whitgift 21 April 1567 – June 1567; died 29 February 1604 (*Handbook of British Chronology*)
John Young 12 July 1567 – 16 March 1578; died 10 April 1605
William Fulke Elected and admitted 10 May 1578 – death; died 28 August 1589
Lancelot Andrewes Elected and admitted 6 September 1589 – 1605; died 25 September 1626
Samuel Harsnett Elected and admitted 9 November 1605; resigned 18 February 1616; died 25 May 1631
Nicholas Felton Elected 29 June 1616; admitted 13 July; resigned 18 February 1619 (letter; resignation accepted 21 February); died 5 October 1626
Jerome Beale Elected 21 February 1619; admitted 23 February 1619; died 1630
Benjamin Lany 25 December 1630, ejected 13 March 1644, restored 1660, resigned 16 August 1662, died 24 January 1675

Richard Vines 22 May 1644; ejected 1650; died 4 February 1656
Sidrach Simpson 1650–5; died April 1655
William Moses April 1655; ejected 1660; died 1688
Mark Franck Elected 23 August 1662, admitted 29 August 1662; died January 1664
Robert Mapletoft c. May 1664, died 20 August 1677 (at the second hour of the morning)
Nathaniel Coga Elected 20 August 1677 ('at the sixth hour of the morning'); admitted **the same day** ('at the eighth hour following'); died 8 January 1694
Thomas Browne Elected 3 February 1694; admitted 10 February 1694; died 9 March 1707
Edward Lany Elected 15 March 1707; admitted 24 March 1707; died 9 August 1728
John Hawkins Elected 15 August 1728; admitted 14 November 1728; resigned 24 September 1733 (resignation recorded in register 10 October 1733); died 1736
Roger Long Elected and admitted 12 October 1733; died 16 December 1770
James Brown Elected 21 December 1770; admitted 22 December 1770; died 30 September 1784
Joseph Turner Elected and admitted 6 October 1784; died 3 August 1828
Gilbert Ainslie Elected and admitted 15 August 1828; died 9 January 1870
John Power Elected and admitted 14 January 1870, died 18 November 1880
Charles Edward Searle Elected and admitted 24 November 1880, died 29 July 1902
Sir George Gabriel Stokes Elected and admitted 12 August 1902; died 1 February 1903
Arthur James Mason Elected and admitted 11 March 1903; resigned 15 June 1912; died 24 April 1928 (DNB)
William Sheldon Hadley Elected and admitted 19 June 1912; died 25 December 1927
Arthur Hutchinson Elected and admitted 16 January 1928; retired 30 September 1937; died December 1937
Sir Montagu Sherard Dawes Butler Pre-elected 9 March 1937; admitted 1 October 1937; retired 31 July 1948; died 1952
Sir Sydney Castle Roberts 1 August 1948; retired 31 July 1958; died 1966
Sir William Vallance Douglas Hodge 1 August 1958; retired 31 July 1970; died 1975
William Anthony Camps 4 August 1970; retired 31 July 1981; died 17 January 1997
Richard Hume Adrian, 2nd Baron Adrian of Cambridge 4 August 1981; retired 30 September 1992; died 4 April 1995
Sir William Roger Tomkys 1 October 1992

Jayne Ringrose

Appendix C: Honorary Fellows

1887–1906	The Right Hon. Sir Edward Thornton
1887–1888	Sir Henry James Sumner Maine
1893–1915	Sir William Rann Kennedy
1899–1927	William Burnside
1900–1907	The Rev. William Haig Brown
1900–1907	Timothy Holmes
1903–1940	The Right Rev. Bishop George Rodney Eden
1911–1936	Sir George Frederic Warner
1911–1949	John Neville Keynes
1912–1928	Canon Arthur James Mason
1920–1926	John Frederick Peel Rawlinson
1924–1927	William Barclay Squire
1924–1937	Sir Montagu Sherard Dawes Butler
1931–1955	Sir Geoffrey Fitzhervey de Montmorency
1938–1957	Sir John Edward Singleton
1941–1982	The Right Hon. Lord Butler
1946–1966	Sir Ernest Henry Pooley
1946–1974	The Right Hon. Sir John William Fisher Beaumont
1949–1965	Sir Pierson John Dixon
1951–1957	Alan John Bayard Wace
1953–1975	Sir Arthur Edward Drummond Bliss
1954–1957	The Most Reverend Geoffrey Hare Clayton
1958–1978	Sir Alexander George Grantham
1958–	The Right Hon. Lord Plowden
1959–1980	Sir George White Pickering
1959–1980	Gordon Brims Black McIvor Sutherland
1962–1971	Harry Frank Guggenheim
1962–1994	Sir Henry Ashley Clarke
1964–1978	Basil Willey
1965–1982	Sir Geoffrey Langdon Keynes
1965–1989	Sir Roger Aubrey Baskerville Mynors
1965–1991	The Right Hon. Lord Salmon
1970–1975	Sir William Vallance Douglas Hodge
1970–1991	The Right Hon. Lord Penney
1973–1987	The Right Hon. Sir David Arnold Scott Cairns
1973–1987	Sir Henry Frank Harding Jones
1973–	Hrothgar John Habakkuk
1975–1996	Sir Patrick Reginald Evelyn Browne
1976–1980	Roy Pascal
1976–1996	Sir Arthur Eric Courtney Drake
1976–1991	Sir John Guthrie Ward
1983–	Sir Michael Francis Atiyah
1983–	Ray Milton Dolby
1983–1985	Rodney Robert Porter
1983–	Sir Robert James Sainsbury
1986–	Edward James Hughes
1988–	The Rev. John Davis McCaughey
1989–	Sir John Frank Charles Kingman
1989–	Robert Kemsley Orr
1992–	The Right Hon. Lord Prior
1992–	Lord Blake
1992–1997	The Right Hon. Lord Taylor
1992–	Sir Henry (Constant Hendrick) de Waal
1992–1995	William Alfred Fowler
1992–	Simon Kirwan Donaldson
1992–	Christopher Jarvis Haley Hogwood
1993–	Sir David Williams
1993–	James Gee Pascoe Crowden
1995–	The Rev. Charles Kingsley Barrett

INDEX